REACHING
READERS

REACHING READERS

Flexible & Innovative Strategies for Guided Reading

Michael F. Opitz and Michael P. Ford

HEINEMANN
Portsmouth, NH

Heinemann
A division of Reed Elsevier Inc.
361 Hanover Street
Portsmouth, NH 03801-3912
www.heinemann.com

Offices and agents throughout the world

The authors and publisher wish to thank those who have generously given permission to reprint borrowed material:

Figure 1.1 is reprinted from *Strategic Learning in the Content Areas* with permission from the Wisconsin Department of Public Instruction, 125 South Webster Street, Madison, WI 53702. Phone: 1-800-243-8782.

Figure 3.1 is reprinted by permission from "Selecting Books for Beginning Readers" by Barbara Peterson in *Bridges to Literacy: Learning From Reading Recovery* edited by Diane DeFord, Carol A. Lyons, and Gay Su Pinnell. Published by Heinemann, a division of Reed Elsevier Inc., Portsmouth, NH. The figure originally appeared in *Characteristics of Texts That Support Beginning Readers* published by Ohio State University. Figure copyright © 1988 by Barbara Peterson. All rights reserved.

Figures 4.5 and C-2 are adapted by permission of Juliet Sisnroy, Pueblo, CO.

Figure 4.7 is reprinted from *Summer Success: Reading, Student Response Book, Grade 4.* Text copyright © 2001 by Great Source Education Group, Inc. Reprinted by permission of Great Source Education Group, Inc. All rights reserved.

Figures 5.4, A-1, A-2, A-4, A-7, A-8, A-10, and A-11 were originally published in *Flexible Grouping In Reading: Practical Ways to Help All Students Become Better Readers* by Michael F. Opitz. Published by Scholastic Professional Books. Copyright © 1998 by Michael F. Opitz. Reprinted by permission of Scholastic Professional Books.

Figures 5.12 and C-11 are adapted by permission of Brenda Wallace, Ashwaubenon, WI.

Figure 5.13 is adapted by permission of Kim Brown, Oshkosh, WI.

Credit lines continue on p. vi.

Library of Congress Cataloging-in-Publication Data
Opitz, Michael F.
   Reaching readers / flexible and innovative strategies for guided reading / Michael F. Opitz and Michael P. Ford.
     p. cm.
   Includes bibliographical references and index.
   ISBN 0-325-00358-0 (paper)
   1. Guided reading. I. Ford, Michael P. II. Title.

LB1050.377 .O65 2001
372.41'62—dc21   2001026410

Editor: Lois Bridges
Production: Lynne Reed
Cover design: Cathy Hawkes, Cat & Mouse Design
Manufacturing: Steve Bernier

Printed in the United States of America on acid-free paper
05 04 03 02 01 ML 1 2 3 4 5

Continued from p. iv.

Contents

List of Figures

Acknowledgments

During a time in which many are willing to criticize and few express their appreciation for teachers, I would like to acknowledge the many wonderful Wisconsin educators with whom I have worked over the years. They have been generous in opening their districts and classrooms so that I could observe, support, and provide the very best in reading instruction. They have informed my thinking and changed my ideas about what the best practices in reading should be.

I would like to express specific appreciation to Neva Hodge Lemorande, Mary Grafenstein, and Evelyn Gundersen (School District of Elkhart Lake–Glenbeulah); Kathy Ruh, Melody Manion, and Donna Van Boxtel (Appleton Area School District); Tom Leuschow (Jefferson School District); Heidi Mumm (Oconomowoc School District); Vicki Wright (Fort Atkinson School District); Jo Pirlott and Kathy Champeau (Muskego-Norway School District); Stacy Sheridan-Clark and Albert Graham (Neenah School District); Patti Vickman, Kim Ott, and Kim Brown (Oshkosh Area School District); Jill Plashko (Wee Wisdom Preschool); Diane Bushkie (Hustisford School District); Joan Larson and Brenda Wallace (Ashwaubenon School District); Jodi Straub and Kathy Parish (Fond du Lac School District); and Millie Hoffman, Linda Gehrig, Mary Schulman, and Flo Pearson (Milwaukee Public Schools). Special thanks go to the teachers and staff of Amity Elementary School in the Waupun School District—Lynn Opperman, Mary Anne Zimmerlee, Deb Witthun, Karol Harmsen, Marilyn Klobuchar, Wayne Jahns, Jean Tenpas, Nancy Davis, Lou Havlik, and Cheri Rens—who made it so easy for me to descend the Ivory Tower and spend a year teaching in a first-grade classroom again.

I would also like to acknowledge the support of the University of Wisconsin Oshkosh in all my professional endeavors, especially Dean Carmen Coballes-Vega and my colleagues in the Reading Department—Judy Lambert, Margaret Genisio, Joan Simmons, Brenda Shearer, and Pat Scanlan. Thanks also to the ongoing support of my "family" in the Wisconsin State Reading Association, to Sandra Wilde for first bringing my work to the attention of Heinemann editor Lois Bridges, and to Lois for her enthusiasm for this project.

—Michael Ford

As with other publications, so many individuals have provided a wealth of insight and support throughout the writing of this book. I would especially like to acknowledge my editor, Lois Bridges, for her prompt, specific suggestions and, as important, for her encouragement and reassurance. Specific appreciation to my son, Josh, for his clerical work; to the many teachers who helped me to see the need for a text such as this; to Juliet Sisnroy and Danette Williams for their lesson designs, which are shown in Chapter 4; and to the individuals at Heinemann who transformed the manuscript into this book. My sincere thanks to each of you.

—Michael F. Opitz

Introduction

I just have to know," a teacher insisted. "Is guided reading appropriate for third graders? I mean, I heard that guided reading is supposed to end at third grade and literature circles are to replace it."

"What do you think guided reading is?" I responded.

She continued, "I think it's a time when the teacher works with small groups of kids who need help in becoming independent readers."

"Are there third graders who need help with this?" I replied.

"There sure are in my classroom!"

"Then I guess you've answered the question. Of course guided reading can be useful in third grade! In fact, using literature circles is one way to guide readers."

So the conversation ended, but questions about guided reading have only intensified. In fact, the questions teachers continue to ask convinced us of the need for this book. Frequently, we encounter teachers who believe that there is just one way to do guided reading, and they want our verification that they are doing it *the* right way. Could it be that guided reading has become an orthodoxy with a set of defined guidelines that teachers think they must follow religiously?

True, *guided reading*—the practice of meeting with readers to provide focused reading instruction—is increasingly perceived as an integral part of a balanced reading program designed to help all children become independent readers. The fact that guided reading is being promoted and implemented by many classroom teachers is no surprise. It gives teachers greater opportunities to provide instruction that more effectively scaffolds learning and engages all learners. Guided reading also enables critical, strategic coaching.

Seems straightforward enough but it's clear many teachers have many questions about what is the best way to do guided reading. Indeed, you may have picked up this book because you were wondering:

- What is meant by guided reading?
- Is there only one way to do guided reading?

- What are the essentials of guided reading?
- What criteria do I use to form groups?
- How many students should be in a group?
- How often do I change the groups' members?
- How do I select the books?
- Should I choose new or familiar texts?
- What should I do during the guided reading lesson?
- Does guided reading change when I work with older students? If so, how does it change?
- What should the rest of the class do when I am working with guided reading groups?
- How do I keep track of what everyone is doing?

As these questions show, effectively implementing guided reading is complex. One way to unravel this complexity is to take a look at each of these questions in depth, which is the purpose of this book. Our goal is to help you—novice and veteran teachers alike—to better understand guided reading and its many exciting possibilities for breakthrough instruction. Based on what we now know about guided reading, we can reflect on how to make it an even more effective and efficient instructional technique to ensure that all students maximize their potential as independent, lifelong readers. Indeed, this reflection makes reaching readers more likely.

In Chapter 1, we provide a definition of guided reading and take a look at the essentials of guided reading instruction. Is there one right way to do guided reading? Absolutely not! Like others who write on this topic, we believe that there are critical elements for any instruction that carries the guided reading label. At the same time, however, our classroom experiences, working with numerous teachers, and reading what others have written have helped us to see that there are many procedures to engage students in guided reading experiences. Each calls for a different way to group children and to structure what happens when they partici- pate in the guided reading experience. Even with children who are just learning to read, there is more than one way to do guided reading. The rationale for our expanded view of guided reading is underscored in this book's first chapter.

Chapter 2 focuses on questions about how guided reading groups are formed. We address concerns about size, number, and group membership. This discussion includes how to use the results of assessment strategies as well as the kind of guided reading experience we want to provide to form groups. We also discuss just how often the groups should change. Like- wise, keeping groups fluid is central to this explanation, because this is one attribute that makes present-day guided reading different from the small-group instruction of the past. Without this flexibility—which we are beginning to see time and again—the negative consequences of past practices are sure to resurface.

Chapter 3 provides answers to questions about selecting texts for guided reading experiences. The main idea of the chapter is that there are many different types of reading materials and several ways to match readers to them. You should decide which text to use depending on your purpose for the guided reading experience. The chapter provides sample titles and suggestions for using each type of text.

In Chapter 4, we visit nine different classrooms to "show" guided reading in action. The chapter describes and explains the five considerations that underscore purposeful guided reading experiences; they are all at play in each of the classroom vignettes.

What children do on their own when they are not working with teachers is the focus of Chapter 5. We suggest that the power of instruction away from the teacher is just as important as the power of instruction with the teacher. Thus, in this chapter, we present ideas for keeping children meaningfully engaged, which will free you up to interact with guided reading groups with minimal interruptions. We also offer some easy-to-use recordkeeping strategies that may yield helpful information that can be used to inform and instruct and provide accountability.

The book closes with appendices that you can use to extend the text in one way or another. We have included forms as well as additional bibliographies.

Keep in mind that the focus of this book is guided reading—one of several components of a more comprehensive literacy program. If you think of all the elements of a literacy program as performers on a stage, imagine guided reading stepping forward to sing the lead while other elements remain in the background to provide the necessary harmony that rounds out the performance. Explanations of these elements are left to other books.

Success breeds success for student and teacher alike. With this in mind, we encourage you to take time to celebrate your successes in reaching readers through guided reading.

CHAPTER ONE

Roles and Goals

To understand guided reading, let's draw an analogy to a mosaic. Although we may study each tile that comprises a mosaic, when we examine the mosaic as a whole we realize that each piece works in concert with the others to create a complex work of art. So it is with guided reading. First discussed by Betts in 1946, guided reading caught our attention in the early 1990s when Margaret Mooney addressed it in her book *Reading To, With, and By Students* (1990). Since then, many others have defined guided reading (Calkins, 2000; Cunningham et. al., 2000; Fountas & Pinnell, 1996, 2001; Routman, 2000; Smith & Elley, 1994). While each perspective has merit in its own right, exploring what they have in common helps us understand the present vision of guided reading. As Loban commented years ago (1976): "Complex truth is always an aggregate; each of us offers only a part of an evolving mosaic."

In this chapter, we address the following questions, define our view of guided reading, and explain the reasons for our perspective.

- Just what is guided reading?
- What do those who currently write about guided reading have in common with regard to this important instructional practice?
- How might their perspectives differ?
- What works with guided reading and what needs revisiting?

We begin with this examination and explanation to guard against a "guided reading dogma." We need to be cautious when an educational practice, like guided reading, begins to develop the trappings of an orthodoxy. We've seen it happen with other educational practices such as cooperative learning, process writing, and word walls. A *one-size-fits-all* viewpoint begins to shape practice, and teachers find themselves struggling to make the "conventional wisdom ideal" fit their unique contexts and classrooms. We embrace John Dewey's wisdom: "Any theory and set of practices is dogmatic which is not based upon critical examinations of its own underlying principles" (1938, p. 22). We believe the time has come to take a critical look at what has evolved into the practice called *guided reading*.

Just What Is Guided Reading, Anyhow?

While those who write about guided reading interpret its subtle complexities somewhat differently, all agree that guided reading is planned, intended, focused instruction. Usually in small-group settings, teachers help students learn more about the reading process. What's more, everyone also believes that the ultimate goal is to foster independent readers, and that guided reading is a means to this end rather than the end itself.

Understandings About Guided Reading

The following sections descibe other common elements of guided reading.

■ *All children have the ability to become literate.*
Every child is ready to learn something. As teachers, our job is to determine what the child is ready to learn and to design instruction accordingly.

■ *To maximize their full reading potential, all children need to be taught by skilled teachers.*
Good teaching matters every step of the way. This is especially true for the children who need help the most. Snow et al. (1998) have these comments:

> Children who are having difficulty learning to read do not, as a rule, require qualitatively different instruction from children who are "getting it." Instead, they more often need application of the same principles by someone who can apply them expertly to individual children who are having difficulty for one reason or another (p. 12).

Teacher demonstrations, modeling, explanations, and encouragement—all of which can happen during guided reading—are powerful techniques that can take children to new heights.

■ *The goal of guided reading is to help children become independent readers.*
As stated earlier, guided reading is a means to an end rather than the end itself. The whole purpose of providing children with guided reading experiences is to help them become independent readers as quickly as possible. In Routman's (2000) words, "the final goal is not guided reading; it is to enable students to become independent readers who comprehend, analyze, problem solve, and self-monitor as they read and choose to read for pleasure and information" (p. 140).

■ *Guided reading is but one component of an effective reading program.*
The purpose of guided reading is to show children how to read and to provide a scaffold (i.e., support) for them as they read. An effective literacy program also includes reading aloud by the teacher, shared reading (i.e., reading an enlarged text together as a class), and independent reading by students.

■ *Reading for meaning is the primary goal of guided reading.*
True, instruction will provide insights and may focus on points other than meaning, but meaning is still the primary objective. Instruction is designed to help children construct meaning. Years ago, Betts (1946) noted:

> During the first reading the child is encouraged to ask for any kind of help he needs. To stimulate interest, to enlist effort, and to cause the child to come to grips with the meaning, this silent reading is guided by suggestions, comments, and questions (p. 508).

■ *Children learn to read by reading.*
To become competent readers, they need to do a lot of reading at their independent and instructional levels (Allington 2001; Krashen, 1993). There is general agreement that when children read with 95 to 100 percent word accuracy and 75 to 100 percent comprehension, they are reading at their *independent* level. Because they can identify nearly every word with ease, their reading sounds fluent and they are more apt to show greater understanding. When children read with 91 to 94 percent word accuracy and 60 to 75 percent comprehension, they are reading at their *instructional* level. At this level, they need help with a few words and they read with some understanding.

■ *Children need to become metacognitive: knowing what they know—the why and how of reading.*
Children need to become aware of how reading works, and they need to be able to use this knowledge to make the reading process work for them. This is called *metacognition* (McNeil, 1987). Research shows that when children are aware of their reading behaviors, they make good progress (Brown & Palinscar, 1982; Paris, 1983; Raphael, 1982; Wong & Jones, 1982).

   Pressley (1998) found that exemplary teachers—those who had the greatest impact on primary students' performance and achievement—promoted this self-regulation. When teachers think aloud to demonstrate how they monitor their own reading behaviors, children are able to better understand how competent readers control reading. As a result, children are more likely to develop similar knowledge about their own reading

(Davey, 1983). This is one reason it is so important for students to work in reading groups with others who might be able to provide them with new insights into the reading process. This is less likely to happen if students are always grouped with readers who share their same knowledge base.

■ *To be independent readers, children need to develop a self-extending system.*
One of the ways to nurture students as independent readers is to question and model specific reading strategies. For example, to show students the importance of attending to visual and meaning clues when they come to an unknown word, the teacher can say something like, "I need a word that begins with 's' that makes sense." This guidance leads children to internalize specific strategies they can use independently to successfully read a text. Once internalized, they can use whichever strategy they feel is the best to help them solve the problem at hand. Most often, one strategy does not work in all situations; the students are able to monitor themselves and choose from a range of strategies because they have developed a "self-extending system" (Clay, 1991).

■ *All children need to be exposed to higher-level thinking activities.*
All of the following tasks call on students to think about what they have read and to make connections with themselves, their world, and other texts.

■ Learning how to retell story events either orally or in writing
■ Discussing important events in a specific reading selection
■ Listening and responding to others' views of a given reading selection
■ Rereading text to find evidence to support a point of view

As such, these are often considered higher-level thinking activities because students must go beyond the surface level of the text. Renzulli (1998) reminds us that

> all students should have opportunities to develop higher-order thinking skills, to pursue more rigorous content than is typically found in today's "dumbed-down" textbooks, and to undertake firsthand investigations (p. 106).

■ *Children need to experience joy and delight as a result of the reading experience.*
One of the main goals of providing children with different guided reading experiences is to show them that reading can be enjoyable and something they would want to do on their own. We not only teach children to read, but we also teach children to be readers. As they have success with specific texts, children most often want to repeat the experience, which provides meaningful, purposeful practice that leads to a favorable view of reading (Gambrell, 1996; Opitz, 1995; Watson, 1997).

■ *Specific elements characterize the successful guided reading lesson.*
As the teacher, you might do the following:

■ Rely on a three-part lesson plan: before/during/after reading. Use specific teaching strategies at each phase of the lesson to help children achieve independence.
■ Determine one focal point (i.e., purpose) for each lesson.
■ Direct every guided reading lesson; that is, it is a time for you to directly teach students something specific about reading.
■ Choose a variety of books and other printed matter to ensure that your students learn how to read different genres.
■ Devote the majority of the guided reading lesson to independent reading, helping children read their own books or other reading materials.
■ Assist individual children as needed. You also can use this time to informally assess individual students.
■ Emphasize teaching points, such as how to reread to identify an unknown word or how to look at pictures or diagrams to help gain meaning from text, that often surface as children "work" the text (Watson, 1997). Therefore, when children have finished reading, you sometimes do a short lesson (i.e., minilesson) that is related to the teaching point.
■ Recognize that comprehension is the essence of reading and the importance of making sure that students gain this understanding. It helps if you also engage children in a discussion about what they read.
■ Conduct ongoing assessments to determine what children know and what they need to know. Sometimes this assessment can be informal; for example, during a literature discussion, you could record how each child interacted and what each one contributed. At other times, the assessments can be more formal. For example, you may ask students to retell a story and use a protocol form to record what students were able to retell.

What Are the Different Guided Reading Perspectives?

Although there are common understandings that are the foundation for guided reading, there are also differences among those who write about guided reading. The following list describes the differences that influence how teachers can use this instructional practice.

1. *Text selection:* While all agree that texts need to be selected for guided reading instruction, some believe that the teacher should control selection whereas others believe that there is a place for student selection.
2. *Number of titles:* Several authors who write about guided reading maintain that every child in the group needs to read the same title (a

"six-pack" takes on new meaning here!). Others suggest that there are times the members of a guided reading group can read a variety titles. While the titles may differ, often all books address the same topic.

3. *Format:* Small-group instruction is generally synonymous with guided reading. However, there are those who believe that guided reading can happen in a variety of formats. For example, you might begin a lesson with the entire class, then break students into small groups that you guide, only to come back together as a whole class to discuss what was learned.

4. *Grouping students:* Many proponents of guided reading talk about grouping students who are similar in their ability level, a strategy that resembles homogeneous grouping. Others emphasize that children can and should be grouped in a variety of ways based on needs, interests, authors, and/or genres.

5. *The role of the teacher:* While some view the teacher as the director of the lesson, others view the teacher as a group member. At these times, the teacher facilitates the discussion, often providing his or her insights, with the children.

What Works with Guided Reading?

As one component of a larger balanced literacy program, guided reading has much to offer. It enables teachers to work with groups of children, thereby learning more about them as they plan instruction accordingly. Guided reading also affords children with more opportunities to interact with each other and the teacher. As a result of this interaction, students are more likely to understand both the text and what it means to engage in a discussion (Gambrell & Almasi, 1996). Children also begin to understand that reading is as much a social activity as it is an isolated one (Yinger & Hendricks-Lee, 1993; Griffin, 2001).

How Might We Revisit and Revise Guided Reading?

As with any education practice, the more we use guided reading, the more we learn about it. We discover ways we can revise, refine, and expand our vision as we reflect on our practice. In this way, we continue to add to our understanding of the guided reading mosaic. As guided reading continues to grow in popularity, so does our concern about its implementation. Indeed, there are five specific concerns, which we describe next.

Instructional Format

When we attend professional conferences, we hear comments like, "Struggling readers need to experience guided reading every day. They should participate in literature circles but not as often as the other children." If we want to instill a love of reading and an accurate view of what it means to be a reader, this statement is unsettling if not alarming. Literature circles are an excellent way to provide guided reading. What we propose is an alternative vision to this either/or proposition: Either I use guided reading or I use literature circles. We propose that the current vision of guided reading be expanded so that it is broad enough to include literature circles and other grouping formats.

Grouping

Another concern relates to the many times we have seen children placed in groups based on the number of words they can read accurately from a given passage or text (i.e., running record). Little attention is given to *how* the accuracy score was actually achieved; yet, taking time to understand this can lead to different groupings within a classroom. That is, some children achieve accuracy by focusing on how words actually look, while others focus on meaning. Still other times, children notice that they have misread a word and reread to fix it (i.e., self-correct). In other words, children with the same accuracy score may very well need different kinds of instruction.

Clay (1993) presents a classic example of this when she describes how two different children read *The Bicycle*. One student misses four words, substituting "lake" for "lady," "box" for "boy," "bil" for "bicycle," and "square" for "squashed." The second student misses four words, substituting "girl" for "lady," "man" for "boy," "bike" for "bicycle," and "flat" for "squashed." In terms of their accuracy score, both students look exactly the same. But a careful examination of their miscues provides further insight into the students' differing needs. Guided reading practices that group children according to accuracy are more likely to mismatch appropriate instruction and student needs.

Overreliance on Accuracy Scores

We must acknowledge our concern that an overreliance on accuracy scores can be problematic; sometimes accuracy scores are anything but accurate. Misinterpreting accuracy can lead to inaccurate assumptions about children followed by an inappropriate instructional response. Consider, for example, a child who reads a repetitive story and substitutes "a" for "the" every time "the" is seen. According to running-record scoring procedures, this miscue must be counted as an error every time it occurs. Therefore, when doing the calculations to determine accuracy, this book may appear to be beyond the child's reading level when, in fact, it is not. In this case, the accuracy score is incidental (Traill, 1993).

What About Comprehension?

If we take a close look at the preceding example, we see that substituting "a" for "the" did not change the meaning of the text; the child was showing signs of paying attention to meaning, substituting the general article for the specific article. If we place children in groups primarily according to their accuracy scores, then children may get inappropriate instruction. Likewise, if we rarely engage children in discussions to determine what they are taking away from the reading experience and what they actually comprehend, they are left with the impression that reading means saying words accurately.

Our flexible view of guided reading makes it clear that both accuracy and comprehension determine a reader's instructional reading level (see p. 9). As discussed before, we have rarely seen this occur. When both measures are used, more weight is often given to how well students read words rather than to their comprehension of them and the text as a whole. Sometimes, the two scores are averaged to determine an overall level. Children are then grouped by *ability*—those who attained the same overall score. A closer look at scores, however, reveals that children need to be grouped differently depending on the focus of the lesson. If teaching a given comprehension strategy is the focus, those children who need to learn it can be grouped together. If the focus is on helping children acquire additional reading vocabulary, students would be grouped accordingly.

Text Selection

The final concern here relates to current efforts to level and match texts and readers. Conventional wisdom suggests that we can do better at reaching readers when we choose reading material that is within their reach. We certainly agree that learners are aware of the potential for success and that the effort to match texts and readers makes sense. But we also must remember that this process is anything but simple. The interaction among texts, readers, and reading contexts is highly complex and involves a number of variable factors (see Chapter 3). We need to be cautious about labeling readers and texts in terms of levels. Additionally, we need to understand that matching a reader to a text is more complicated than bringing together a text and reader at a given level.

The danger in this current effort manifests itself in the way both texts and readers are perceived. Imagine that every text in a classroom is leveled, labeled, and placed in some kind of box or basket. The level of the book, then, may take on an artificial importance—what counts about the books is not the authors, topics, titles, or formats, it's the level! We are concerned that book selection may center on levels while more important factors, such as personal interest, take a backseat. Will access to certain books at higher levels now become restricted to some? Will the acceptability of books at lower levels become less desirable to others?

Now, imagine that every student in a classroom is leveled and labeled, and that the grouping decisions are made exclusively around those levels and labels. Would it surprise you to learn that the children have begun to label themselves according to their levels and to perceive their abilities in terms of how they compare with the levels and labels of others? What's more, some children may begin to doubt their own abilities because of these social comparisons. When children are asked to talk about themselves as readers and they only talk about their guided reading levels, we need to reexamine our practices!

Likewise, when readers are asked to evaluate themselves as readers and they talk primarily about how their reading level compares to others, we must reconsider our guided reading practices lest we find ourselves repeating the mistakes of the past. Many of us can recall the negative impact of ability grouping, either as teachers or as students who were forced to endure the stigma of the "low" group.

Clearly, there are many dimensions to understanding how to use guided reading as a vehicle to help children become independent readers.

So, What Is Our View of Guided Reading?

While our guided reading perspective encompasses many commonly accepted understandings, we recommend a wide array of experiences to open up new learning possibilities for teachers and students alike. There is definitely more than one way to do guided reading. Each guided reading experience calls for alternative ways to group children; that is, having all children read a copy of the same text is but one of several options for effective guided reading instruction. We believe our flexible view of guided reading is essential. Our reasons for an expanded view are discussed in the following sections.

What It Means to Be a Reader

All children need to understand that the primary purpose for reading is understanding. They also need to understand that some texts are easier to read than others and that this challenge is based on many factors, including the reader's interest in the topic (Almasi, McKeown, & Beck, 1996; Reed & Schallert, 1993), the reader's background knowledge of the subject (Alexander, 1996), and the author's writing style.

For example, as adults, we rarely label ourselves as readers in terms of levels. Instead, when we engage in conversations about reading, we typically talk about the books we are reading. Our view of guided reading addresses the concern that too much emphasis on a book's level causes children to define themselves as a "level" rather than as a reader who can engage with a particular text.

Taken to the extreme are those schools in which every title in the library and classroom is leveled either with a number or a colored dot. The number is often given as much weight as the title of the book. Indeed, the level may be printed on the outside front cover alongside the title, author, and illustrator. This can be unfortunate. Consider the following scenario that a reading teacher recently related to us. In approaching a boy with whom he had worked in the past, the teacher stopped to ask, "So, what are you reading?" The student replied, "Level 11." Probing further, the teacher asked, "What is your goal for reading?" To which the student replied, "To get to level 12."

The student never mentioned titles or authors; his singular focus on level saddened and concerned his teacher. Our flexible view of guided reading enables us to avoid the "days of old" when students defined their reading abilities based solely on level and comparisons with their peers.

How Children Develop as Readers

When we think of how children develop as readers, we think of lightning strikes rather than straight lines. Smith and Elley (1994) echo our view, commenting: "The reality is that there is no orderly progression—children's understanding of print does not develop in a linear fashion" (p. 29). A child might very well be reading a book that we consider well beyond his or her level one day and the next day struggle with an on-level book.

This is so because there are many factors that contribute to the successful reading of a text (as shown in Figure 1.1); some relate to the text (e.g., difficulty level, genre, format), whereas others relate to the reader (e.g., background knowledge, interest). Still other factors relate to the context in which the reading occurs (e.g., makeup of classroom, physical environment, task expectations). The interaction of these variables accounts for the relative success of each particular reading experience (Alexander & Jetton, 2000; Leslie & Jett-Simpson, 1997). Our view of guided reading challenges the notion that success is ensured by simply matching a child to a specific text level. It acknowledges the complexity of variables that intersect when an individual comprehends.

Expanding the Ability to Develop Self-Extending Systems

Most educators understand the importance of helping children become independent readers. As noted earlier, one of the ways this is accomplished is to help children develop a "self-extending system" (Clay, 1991). That is, children learn to internalize specific strategies they can use independently to successfully read a text. For example, students might be taught how "chunking" a longer word enables them to find smaller, meaningful parts to use in figuring out the whole word.

So it is with us as teachers. Rather than having one way to think about guiding children through texts, we learn that there are several types of guided reading experiences. Thinking through our many options leads to decisions about the best teaching strategies to use as well as which texts to use and the way to group the children for the experience.

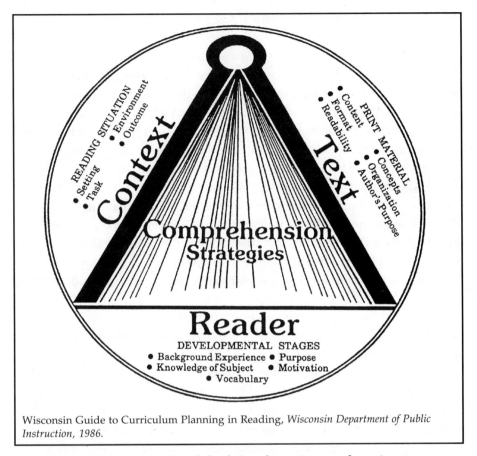

Wisconsin Guide to Curriculum Planning in Reading, *Wisconsin Department of Public Instruction, 1986.*

FIGURE 1.1 Wisconsin Model of Reading Comprehension

Enable Teachers to Expand Their Use of Effective Practices

Much research has revealed that grouping children by ability is fraught with problems; for reviews of these studies, see Barr, 1995; Caldwell and Ford, 1996; and Opitz, 1998. However, because many teachers have subscribed to a view of guided reading that emphasizes the use of text levels (i.e., simple rhyming and/or repetitive books with supportive pictures for lower levels, then increase in difficulty as some features are replaced by more complicated text and fewer pictures) as the primary way to group children, what we frequently see is a return to ability grouping.

When we rely on such groupings for guided reading, we are apt to revisit the problems of the past. For example, teachers wear themselves out trying to meet with several guided reading groups each day; children are placed in groups solely for management purposes; and, as in the past, children spend too much time away from the teacher. Often students are just doing tasks designed to keep them busy while the teacher works with a small group. Our view of guided reading invites teachers to use the best of what is known about the value of grouping while avoiding the pitfalls of ability grouping.

The Nature of Acceptable Texts Used for Guided Instruction

Many different types of texts can be used for guided reading experiences (see Chapter 3). Without question, we want guided reading experience texts children can read with relative ease so that time can be spent on the specific teaching point—learning about an author's style; a literary element, such as the setting of a story; or a specific reading strategy. Yes, commercial leveled texts, which have been written to use during guided reading (e.g., little books), can be used, but in more than one way. The way texts are used will depend on the purpose of the guided reading experience. For example, if the purpose of the guided reading experience is to talk about the setting of a story, the text's level can vary according to the children in the group. In this case, level is not as important because the focus will be on a literary element. Likewise, a teacher may choose to use a single title with all children within the group, regardless of their perceived level.

For one reason or another, teachers often feel compelled to use leveled texts that are part of a larger reading program as the mainstay in their approach to guided reading. In fact, they are sometimes led to believe that they must use these texts in order to do guided reading the proper way. For example, when attending a standing-room only session about using nonfiction for guided reading, the presenters indicated that the best way to help children read nonfiction was to use the nonfiction readers they were explaining and selling. It is no surprise, then, that teachers sometimes think of guided reading in terms of specific texts. They may even feel disenfranchised; as one teacher exclaimed, "I'd do guided reading but I don't have those leveled little books."

As shown in Chapter 3, commercial leveled texts are but one type of printed matter that can be used for guided reading experiences; there are many additional types. For example, you can choose children's literature, which is sometimes overlooked, for guided reading experiences. Recognizing this liberates you from having to rely on a given guided reading program. Therefore, should funds be limited, you and your students can find quality children's literature at school or public libraries. Again, your purpose for the guided reading lesson is what determines the text or texts you and your students choose and how they will be used throughout the lesson.

Expanding Literacy Growth Using Scaffolding

Scaffolding enables teachers not only to determine where learners are developmentally, but also where they need to be. Then, teachers can plan sensitive, responsive instruction that will provide a bridge between these two points. Boyle and Peregoy (1998) list five criteria that define the literacy scaffold model. The scaffolds

- are applied to reading and writing activities aimed at functional, meaningful communication found in entire texts such as stories, poems, reports, and recipes;
- make use of language and discourse patterns that repeat themselves and are therefore predictable;
- provide a model, offered by the teacher or by peers, for comprehending and providing particular written language patterns;
- support students in comprehending and producing written language at a level slightly beyond their competence in the absence of the scaffold;
- are temporary and may be dispensed with when the student is ready to work without them (p. 152).

One way of scaffolding learners is to form a text set—books related to a given topic—with specific learners in mind (Opitz, 1998). Children are then grouped by mixed achievement and each child in the group reads a different text related to the topic. Once the children finish reading, they report, talking about their book in one or more ways. The result? All students in the group are exposed to different texts. The children's familiarity with them makes it more likely that they will be able to read the texts by themselves. In other words, texts can sometimes provide a scaffold for other texts as can discussions (Wilkinson & Silliman, 2000).

Another way to provide scaffolded instruction is to group children according to a specific need that the teacher has observed. Children are then taught what they need to know with the support of the teacher. Once the children show understanding, the group dissolves.

Protecting Children from the Debilitating Effects of Labels

Current thinking about how reading develops emphasizes that children progress through stages. Each stage is named and has its own characteristics. For example, *emergent literacy* is sometimes viewed as the first stage (Traill, 1993). Although stages of reading development can be helpful in enabling us to better understand children, they also have the potential of being misused. This is especially true in guided reading. For example, we sometimes read about the best instruction for emergent readers as opposed to those who are in the "early" and "fluent" reading stages. These terms can work to label groups in much the same way the traditional labels (buzzards, bluebirds, and redbirds) of years past did.

Drawing from the work of Vygotsky and our personal experiences, we recognize that one of the best ways to advance ourselves is to collaborate with those who are more capable (Wertsch, 1985). We can learn a lot from them. This is true for readers as well. Focusing on how readers are alike across stages rather than targeting their differences all of the time ensures that children will benefit from interaction with different classmates who can help them discover what it means to be a competent reader.

As Traill's (1993) descriptors of the stages show, regardless of where children are according to her continuum—emergent, early, or fluent—there are commonalities. For example, children in all three stages (1) enjoy listening to stories, (2) choose to read from various resources, (3) retell stories, (4) read to gain understanding, and (5) use pictures as clues. When we acknowledge and celebrate commonalities, we avoid viewing a developmental stage as a discrete variable and defining students solely in terms of reading stages.

Guarantee That Children Get Appropriate Instruction

All children need opportunities to engage with authentic literature (i.e., literature that can be purchased in bookstores and is available in libraries) in a variety of ways (Allington, 2001; Snow et al., 1998). Guided reading can be one of the best ways to provide these opportunities. If the focus of the guided reading experience is to introduce children to a given author, all children benefit. If the purpose of the guided reading experience is to demonstrate how to lead or participate in group discussions, all children are afforded this opportunity. Clearly, students need to be provided with varied learning opportunities associated with becoming independent lifelong readers.

Guided reading can help students advance as readers. To better ensure that all children benefit from guided reading, though, we need to use the procedures associated with it to their best advantage. This means expanding your ideas about what can happen during guided reading instruction. We must view the many discrete parts of guided reading as a mosaic and understand the ways in which the parts contribute to an overall vision of the guided reading experience. An expanded understanding of guided reading provides an instructional tool that will more effectively nurture and support both reading and readers. In sum, there is more than one way to implement guided reading!

CHAPTER TWO

Assessment and Grouping

Grouping children in meaningful ways while at the same time paying attention to potential pitfalls is a complex task. Given this complexity, we are not surprised by the number and type of questions about grouping that surface when we work with teachers.

Frequently, we hear questions like the following:

- How do I decide which children to put into which groups?
- How many groups do I need?
- How large should the groups be?
- How often should I change the groups?

Our reply, "It depends!" is often met with disappointment. Although our response can be unsettling for any person looking for the one *right* answer to these questions, it is the most accurate way to respond. Our teaching experiences, and subsequent investigations, have enabled us to see that there is no one right way to group children for guided reading instruction.

One's purpose needs to guide grouping decisions. This chapter focuses on questions that need to be addressed to organize groups for powerful guided reading instruction. As you read through our responses to the preceding questions, an important point to keep in mind is that the end goal for any grouping decision is providing access to quality instruction for all students.

What Role Does Assessment Play in Grouping Decisions?

Any decision about how to best help children advance as readers through the use of guided reading instruction begins with understanding what students know and what they need to know. Initial observations of students in a variety of contexts—independent reading, reading conferences, large group instruction—and in a variety of content areas will provide logical starting points for guided reading instruction. The observations could be done using specific informal assessment techniques. As we begin to understand students better, we can adjust instruction to reflect what has been learned, reaching all readers as a result.

Although a comprehensive explanation about the best way to assess students is beyond the scope of this book, the sections that follow describe some common measures that can be used to inform guided reading instruction.

Notebooks for Recording Observations

Index Card Folders—Arrange index cards in a file folder as shown. On each side write a student name on the part of the card that shows. Use the cards to record the date and your observation.

FIGURE 2.1. Observation instruments

Observation

Perhaps one of the easiest and least intrusive ways to understand how students approach reading is to watch and listen to them read and to record your observations in one way or another. Some teachers use a three-ring notebook with a section for each child. As the teacher watches students engaged with their books, he or she records observations about their reading behaviors and attitudes. Other teachers use a grid large enough to hold stick-on notes for each child. As they observe, they write notes to place on the grid. (Still other teachers do the same on mailing labels.) Once information has been recorded about given children, the notes or labels are affixed to a sheet of paper with each child's name. These notes are often assembled in an observation notebook (see Figure 2.1, top). Another style of observation notebook is shown in Figure 2.1, bottom.

When specific questions are used to guide observations, the information they reveal can be powerful; however, they can be overwhelming if you try to focus on too many at once. We suggest using one or two questions at a time to make observations both realistic and revealing. Figure 2.2 provides some questions to get you started.

Questions to guide observations for primary grades

- How does the student handle books?
- Does the student attend to print or pictures?
- Does the student have a sense of story?
- Does the student focus on meaning when reading or listening to a story being read aloud?
- Can the student recall or retell what was read?
- Can the student engage in a meaningful discussion with others about a given text?
- Does the student appear interested in reading?
- Does the student appear to have a good attitude about reading?

Questions to guide observations for intermediate grades

- Does the student read for meaning?
- If meaning is not maintained, what does the child do?
- What does the child do when approaching unfamiliar text?
- Does the student adjust his or her rate of reading relative to the purpose for reading the material?
- How well can the student recall or retell what was read?
- Can the student engage in a meaningful discussion with others about a given text?
- Does the student appear interested in what she or he is reading?
- Does the student appear to have a good attitude about reading?

FIGURE 2.2 Questions to guide observation

Informal Assessment Strategies

Although focused observations can be revealing, several other informal measures can be used to show what children do when they read. With so many assessment methods available, choosing one may seem a daunting task. Plus, there is always the danger of assessing too much and teaching too little. Keep in mind that the whole purpose of assessment is to inform instruction; rather than assessing for the sake of assessing, we need to determine what we want to know and why we want to know it. Only then can we choose the most appropriate assessment technique to discover this information.

Figure 2.3 shows several strategies that can be used to assess reading behaviors for guided reading instruction. Specific administration procedures and reproducible forms are available in Appendix A.

What do I want to know?	*Why* do I want to know it?	*How* can I best discover what I want to know?
Does the student read for meaning?	Comprehension is the goal of reading. I need to know if the student is trying to make sense while reading and after reading.	Running Record (primary grades) Modified Miscue (intermediate grades) Retelling (all grades) Questioning (all grades)
How does the student feel about reading?	Attitude impacts desire to read. Children with a positive attitude are more apt to read for a variety of purposes. Likewise, faulty perceptions about reading can hinder reading advancement. Identifying these perceptions is the first step toward change.	Primary Reading Survey (primary grades, it will need to be read to some children) Reading Attitude Survey (intermediate grades) Student Interview (all grades)
What interests the student?	Interest has a huge bearing on desire to read. Determining interests will help me select books for guided reading as well as for the classroom library.	Interest Inventory (all grades)
What is the student's functional reading level?	Children need to read books of varying difficulty levels to become competent readers. A majority of what they read should be at an easy or just-right level. Knowing these levels will help me select books for guided reading. It will also help me know which teaching strategies to use to provide children with adequate support.	Running Record (grades 1–2) Modified Miscue (grades 3–6)

FIGURE 2.3 The what, why, and how of guided reading assessment

What do I want to know?	Why do I want to know it?	How can I best discover what I want to know?
What strategies does the child use when reading?	Good readers use several strategies when they read rather than relying on one. I need to make sure that students learn to use several strategies to ensure their independence.	Running Record (grades 1–2) Modified miscue (grades 3–6)
To what degree does the child read with fluency and expression?	Fluency and expression or lack thereof can affect comprehension.	Multidimensional Fluency Scale (all grades)
To what degree does the child understand how print functions?	Knowing how print functions to create a text is necessary for effective reading.	Print Concepts (grades 1–2)

FIGURE 2.3 The what, why, and how of guided reading assessment (continued)

How Does Purpose Affect Selection of Guided Reading Experiences?

Once children have been assessed, the next step is to consider the purpose for using guided reading. The results of assessments can be particularly helpful for grouping children for one or more of the four common guided reading experiences. Each one is designed for the following specific purposes.

- Do you want to *demonstrate* a specific skill or strategy? If so, a demonstration guided reading experience is needed.
- Would you rather focus on a specific need that has surfaced as a result of one of the assessments you used? In this case, you would use an *intervention* guided reading experience.
- Do you want to provide children with time to share their responses to a book or books as a way of furthering their comprehension? In this case, you should use the *shared response* guided reading experience.
- Are there times when you want to combine one or more of the first three experiences to help students get the most out of the guided reading lesson? For this, you would use a *combination* guided reading experience.

Figure 2.4 shows these ways of guiding experiences and provides descriptions and examples that show when each might be used. Chapter 4 contains specific teaching scenarios that show how these play out. Clearly, each of the guided reading experiences shown here enable children to develop specific reading skills and strategies. Figure 2.5 highlights each of them.

Demonstration

Description: A demonstration guided reading experience is designed by the teacher to show students how to be better readers. The specific strategy, literary element, or learning behavior is modeled by the teacher for students so that they can better understand how to use it in more independent contexts.

Use when . . . you want to demonstrate a specific word identification or comprehension strategy, how to identify and analyze key literary elements, or classroom procedures/processes to improve learning habits and behaviors.

Example: Showing students how to make connections with what they are reading is an essential comprehension strategy. To help students better understand how to do this, Sheryl uses a think-aloud procedure to demonstrate to small groups of children how to use a graphic organizer to record their connections.

Intervention

Description: An intervention guided reading experience is designed to address a specific need that has become evident from watching and listening to children as they read and write. Children with similar needs are grouped together to make efficient use of instructional time. To assist the students to move from where they are to where they need to be, the teacher focuses less on modeling and more on scaffolding instruction.

Use when . . . you identify a specific skill or strategy you want to teach to the children who need to learn it.

Example: As a result of observing his first graders while reading, Mike notices that there are several children who need to learn how to read in phrases. He groups them together to teach them how to do this. He listens carefully as the children chorally read a common text. He waits patiently for a teachable moment—the point at which word-by-word reading could be easily phrased. When the students encounter dialogue, he asks the students to stop and listen to him repeat the way they read it (word-by-word). He asks them if that is the way people talk. He asks them how someone would say that. He talks about the importance of reading like people talk. He guides them to another place in the story where they can practice what they have discussed. He checks individual students on other parts of the text to see if they can apply what has been taught.

Shared Response

Description: A shared response guided reading experience is designed to enable children, regardless of perceived reading level, to share what they are reading with others. The primary purpose for this type of guided reading experience is to enable children to learn from one another through meaningful, focused discussion. To maximize its potential as a learning experience, this discussion is often provided a structure by the teacher.

Use when . . . you want to encourage students to engage in discussion about a common text or different but related texts (same genre, author, topic, themes) they've been reading.

Example: Pat's fifth graders have been reading different mysteries. She wants to provide students time to talk about their mysteries with one another. She specifically wants students to discuss how their authors use foreshadowing to set up the clues for the mystery. Each student was asked to prepare three examples from their text using small stick-on notes to share in the discussion. She uses the shared response guided reading experience to make this happen.

FIGURE 2.4 Guided reading experiences

Combination

> **Description:** A combination guided reading experience is one in which any combination of the first three experiences are used. How to best help children understand a given aspect of reading is what guides the combination.
>
> **Use when . . .** you want to use any combination of the first three types of guided reading experiences to best help students advance in their reading.
>
> **Example:** As a result of her observations, Susan discovers a need for the majority of students in her class: how to lead group discussions. She selects a group of students to role play a group discussion *demonstrating* both good and not so good examples. With the students, she builds a chart detailing what good discussion sounds like and looks like. Then when students move to their independent discussions in small groups, she drops in on each group to monitor their behaviors *intervening* with reminders based on the class-made chart as needed.

FIGURE 2.4 Guided reading experiences (continued)

Guided Reading Experience/ Strategies	Demonstration	Intervention	Shared Response
Comprehension:			
Activating Background	•	•	•
Summarizing	•	•	•
Analyzing	•	•	•
Synthesizing	•	•	•
Evaluation	•	•	•
Making connections	•	•	•
Visualizing	•	•	•
Predicting	•	•	•
Questioning	•	•	•
Monitoring	•	•	•
Phrasing	•	•	•
Fluency	•	•	•
Expression	•	•	•
Reading different genres	•	•	•
Vocabulary	•	•	•

Figure 2.5. Guided reading experiences and the strategies they develop

What Are Some Grouping Options for Guided Reading?

As noted in Chapter 1, a wealth of research has shown that there are many ways of grouping children for effective instruction and that strict adherence to any one method can be harmful to children. This is especially true when we continually group children who appear to be alike (i.e., ability grouping). Perhaps the best way to guard against the pitfalls of grouping is to consider several options for grouping children and to think in terms of using a variety of grouping arrangements—those that will best help achieve the purpose at hand. Let's begin with some definitions to make what we are talking about in this text clear.

Definitions

When reading about grouping, three terms are sure to surface: ability grouping, mixed ability grouping, and flexible grouping. *Ability grouping* is when children are grouped according to similar levels of achievement based on the results of informal or formal assessment measures. This is sometimes called homogeneous grouping. *Mixed-ability grouping* is when the results of informal or formal measures are used to group children of differing levels of achievement together. This is sometimes called heterogeneous grouping. *Flexible grouping* refers to having students work in a variety of differently mixed groups that are drawn together for a specific purpose. Sometimes the children in these groups are similar in their reading behaviors, and at other times they are diverse.

For purposes of this book, we deliberately use *similar achievement* in place of ability grouping and *mixed achievement* in place of mixed-ability grouping. We do so because we believe, as others do (Allington & Cunningham, 1996), that tapping innate ability is difficult if not impossible. The only conclusion that can be drawn from the different reading measurements is how children actually do on them rather than their potential ability. Therefore, talking about achievement is much more accurate than talking about ability. In addition, we recognize that no two children are alike and that to assume otherwise is faulty thinking. We have taken to heart what Betts noted years ago: "When groupings are made for any activity, the teacher should not assume that homogeneity is assured. In fact, homogeneity is a fiction. Children are no more alike than the proverbial two peas in a pod" (1946, p. 391).

We use the term *flexible grouping* in the same way as it was just defined. In fact, we believe that using a variety of grouping procedures is essential for guided reading instruction. As noted, there are different guided reading experiences and each calls for different grouping options.

How Do We Assign Children to Groups?

Whether we use similar achievement or mixed achievement, we also need to think of how we want to assign children to the guided reading groups. At least three possibilities exsist. At times, children can be assigned to groups at random; at other times, interest can be used to assign them to groups. Of course, students sometimes are assigned to groups according to a specific strength or instructional need. Figure 2.6 lists these three ways of assigning children to groups, shows how and when each type of assignment can be used, and gives specific examples.

Assign by	How	Use When	Example
Random	Completely arbitrary	Placement is primarily for management and for forming groups of equal size.	Students choose a title from a bag of books you circulate and group themselves by like title. There are enough titles to form groups of equal size.
Interest	Students are grouped together by some common interest as determined by informal or formal surveys.	Student interest is the main motivating force for learning about a topic.	Students interested in an author or illustrator are grouped together to learn more about him or her.
Skill and/or instructional need	Students who seem to lack a specific skill or strategy are grouped together.	You want to teach the skill or strategy to those who need to learn it.	Children who seem to need a specific skill or strategy are grouped together to learn them.

FIGURE 2.6 Ways to assign children to groups

Shouldn't We Have One Group for Each Reader Level?

One myth we would like to dispel is that a teacher needs one guided reading group for each level of reader in the classroom. This idea over-emphasizes the value of matching the right text to the right group of readers by taking a very narrow view of using *intervention* for guided reading. It marginalizes other factors that need to be considered when organizing groups, including the other guided reading experiences noted in Figure 2.4.

Categorization of readers and texts into discrete levels for a single instructional purpose denies the complexity of the interactions among readers, texts, and the contexts in which instruction takes place. This view of guided reading also ignores the real constraints under which most teachers operate. The expectation that you could juggle one group for each level of reader in a class of diverse learners sets up an unreal expectation and the potential for failure, frustration, and disappointment.

What Is the Best Group Size?

Another point to consider when grouping students has to do with the group's size. This question rarely warrants a single answer. As Figure 2.7 shows, different size groups have advantages and disadvantages, and all can and should be used to their best advantage. Furthermore, as several of the scenarios in Chapter 4 illustrate, many times group size can and does change throughout the course of a guided reading lesson. Sometimes, the teacher begins with the whole class, proceeds to assign students to small groups of two to five members, and then brings students back together to finish out the lesson.

Group Size	Description	Advantages	Disadvantages	When It Works
Whole Class	Teacher works with the whole class and everyone participates in similar activities. In one way or another, the same text is often read by all students.	■ Builds a community of learners ■ Provides a common knowledge base for all	■ Differentiating instruction is more difficult ■ Some students can get frustrated or bored depending on the level of instruction ■ Students may not interact as planned	■ Different learners are considered when planning instruction ■ All members of the class are provided with a similar experience
Small Group	Groups of two to five students work together to accomplish a given task.	■ Provides for focused instruction ■ Engages more learners ■ Students learn to work with one another	■ Students may not interact ■ Creates a higher noise level ■ Students might be grouped together for too long ■ Student perceptions of group can be negative	■ Group membership changes on a regular basis ■ Students are taught how to respond to one another
Partners	Students are paired up with one another to read text in one or more ways.	■ Stays focused ■ Enables relationships to develop ■ Encourages independent learning so the teacher can help those who need it	■ One of the two students may become too dependent on the other ■ One of the two may dominate	■ Partners are switched on a regular basis ■ Procedures are clearly understood by both
Individual	Students work by themselves and each often reads a different text.	■ Allows students to read at a comfortable level and to develop their own understandings ■ Enables teacher to evaluate individual progress to determine what students know and need to know	■ Can be hard to organize ■ Students may become distracted and/or lose focus ■ Little sense of community	■ Reading is at the appropriate level ■ Students understand procedures ■ An effort is made to bring students back together either as a small or large group to discuss what they've learned

FIGURE 2.7 Group size for guided reading experiences

Of course, the number of students placed in each group will depend on the number of students in the class. Having fewer students in each group means juggling more groups if the class is large. In this case, students are probably spending too much time away from the teacher. On the other hand, more students in each group may mean less groups but it requires more time to manage the groups. In addition, having larger groups calls for more resources and more space. The good news is that if we see group size as something that can be adjusted through the use of flexible grouping, we need not feel stuck with a one-size-fits-all way of defining group size.

How Many Groups Should a Class Have at Any One Time?

There are as many answers to this question as there are teachers. That is, teachers need to determine how many groups are optimal for their class-rooms. Certainly, exclusive use of one large group magnifies the flaws inherent in whole-class instruction. On the other hand, juggling six to eight small groups every day borders on the impossible within the practical constraints of a classroom's schedule, space, and curricular demands. The scenarios described in Chapter 4 provide evidence that the number of groups used at any one time varies depending on the purpose of guided reading, the nature of the texts, the students, and the context in which the instruction happens.

How Long Should Groups Be Kept Together?

One point to consider has to do with the duration of groups—how long should they remain intact? The group should stay together until it has accomplished the purpose for forming it in the first place. Once the group's purpose has been achieved, it should dissolve. As the scenarios in Chapter 4 illustrate, sometimes groups remain together for one day; other times they remain together for up to five days. In our classrooms, groups have remained together for as long as two weeks. One group rarely stays to-gether for an entire year. We agree with Nagel, who notes: "Except for the whole-class group, no group needs to last all year. Change should defi-nitely occur whenever any group is becoming a 'caste'" (2001, p. 118).

Whenever you sense that groups are becoming a bit static, consider how to deliberately shake them up to make them more dynamic. If this isn't done, group assignments begin to feel like permanent sentences and can interfere with even the best instruction, especially for those students who need the most help.

Another point to keep in mind is that groupings can, and often do, change within a lesson. As described before, there can be an ebb and flow

Day	Purpose	Group Size	What Can Happen
Monday	Provide a demonstration guided reading experience	Whole group	Teacher introduces the texts that different groups will be reading. Students talk about what they have in common, write responses in their literature response logs.
Tuesday	Provide a demonstration guided reading experience	Small groups: Students are assigned to similar achievement groups at random but groups are of equal size.	Once in their groups, the teacher engages students with the book by introducing it and providing time for students to read and respond to all or part of it.
Wednesday	Provide an intervention guided reading experience	Small groups (see Tuesday)	Students review where they were and the teacher provides support as students finish reading the text.
Thursday	Provide a shared response guided reading experience	Small groups: Students are assigned to mixed-achievement groups at random but each group has students that are reading different titles.	Students select passages to read and tell about their books. Students also talk about what their books have in common.
Friday	Provide intervention	Individual/Partner	Students select any of the books that they or others have been reading over the week. They can read solo or with a partner. While students are reading, the teacher will conference with individuals and note progress.

FIGURE 2.8 Sample Weekly Plan

in which the teacher begins the guided reading lesson with the whole class, divides students into groups in one way or another, and then calls the whole class back together to close the lesson for the day. As the scenario on page 75 in Chapter 4 shows, this format can be used for a period of days.

At other times, you may decide to initiate different guided reading experiences on different days. For example, you may want to provide intervention experiences three days each week. On these days, students would be assigned to groups according to the skill and/or strategy they need to learn. On the other days, you may want to provide shared response guided reading experiences, so students are assigned to groups either at random or by interest. A sample weekly plan is shown in Figure 2.8. Similarly, flexibility can be seen in teachers' grouping decisions over time as they gradually turn responsibility over to students. Figure 2.9 provides but one example.

Weeks	Grouping Decision/Purpose
1	Whole-class grouping is used to introduce all students to a given title, build community, and provide a foundation for future experiences. Depending on length of the text, a different title might be used each day or every couple of days.
2–3	Small groups are used. Text sets, which contain multiple titles and multiple levels, are used as children read in both similar-achievement groups and mixed-achievement groups. Children are exposed to as many titles as possible as groups and titles shift during these two weeks.
4–5	Individualized reading is emphasized and students are encouraged to self-select titles and read independently while the teacher conferences with each. Children are expected to read as many titles as possible.

FIGURE 2.9 Grouping decisions over time

Clearly, the complex interaction of teachers, students, human resources, material resources, external demands, schedules, and other factors makes every classroom quite unique. This is why answering specific questions about grouping is difficult. When thinking about grouping children for instruction, remember to worry less about looking for magical answers to grouping questions and more about the percentage of time that students are engaged in productive literacy activities. A common thread that pervades our responses to the questions in this chapter is the need for *flexibility* in order to provide quality instruction for *all* students.

CHAPTER THREE

Texts

Questions continue to emerge about the types of texts that can be used for guided reading, and rightly so! Selecting books for guided reading is complex, because the students we teach and the contexts in which we teach are complex. Selecting and using appropriate texts, then, demands that we know students' backgrounds, interests, and finesse with text, texts, and the purposes for bringing the two together. Three questions we hear most often are: Why use a variety of texts? What kinds of texts can be used for guided reading? How does a teacher decide which texts to use for a specific guided reading experience? This chapter addresses these most important questions.

Why Use a Variety of Texts?

In everyday life, people read many different types of texts. What they read depends on several factors, including interest and purpose. Using a variety of texts during guided reading, then, is necessary to help students learn what it means to be a reader. Remember that we are teaching children to be readers rather than merely teaching them to read. Right from the start, children need to be reading books and other works written and illustrated by a variety of authors and illustrators. Descriptions of other reasons for using a variety of texts follow.

1. *To help students understand that different texts are written in different ways.* Stories, for example, are written using a story grammar that includes setting, characters, problem, attempts to solve the problem, and resolution. *Expository text*—text that is written to inform—may encompass sequence of events, a compare/contrast situation, and other text structures. Knowing about the different formats or structures that are used to write texts ensures better comprehension of them (Goldman & Rakestraw, 2000; Muth, 1989).
2. *To expose children to content-specific vocabulary and new concepts.* As a result of reading a variety of texts, students acquire larger vocabular-

ies. For example, when reading an informational article about spiders, students learn words associated with them. Increase in knowledge ensures that better reading will occur (Alexander, 1996).

3. *To capitalize on students' interests.* Some students would rather read informational texts than stories. They delight in learning about specific details related to given topics. Providing children with texts they enjoy motiviates them to read (Almasi et al., 1996; Reed & Schallert, 1993).

4. *To serve as a scaffold.* Because stories are generally easier for students to read than nonfiction, fiction and nonfiction can be paired so that when students are finished reading one they will have a better understanding of the content (Camp, 2000). For example, as a way of helping children understand how trees grow and change, they could first read *Red Leaf, Yellow Leaf*, Ehlert's fiction text (1991), and then read *A Tree Is Growing*, Dorros' nonfiction text (1997). Having acquired an understanding of the material presented in these texts, the reader is then more likely to understand information presented in other books, such as textbooks. Reading texts that all relate to a specific topic is another way to provide scaffolding.

5. *To broaden students' knowledge base.* Good comprehension is dependent on knowledge. If we know something about the topic we are reading about, we are more apt to understand what we read and remember it longer. The reverse is also true. Exposing children to different ideas presented in different texts is a way of broadening their knowledge base (Alexander, 1996; Yopp & Yopp, 2000).

Which Texts Can Be Used for Guided Reading? How Might They be Used?

There are several! For purposes of this book, we have divided them into three broad categories: commercial, trade, and other. *Commercial books* are texts that have been written for a given program. Three types of commercial books exist: little books, basal readers, and textbooks. *Little books* are small books that can be easily held by young children (Peterson, 1991). The books usually are the same size, have a paperback cover, and have few pages. *Basal readers* are grade-level anthologies accompanied by additional materials such as teacher guides, workbooks, and commercially created tests. *Textbooks* are books written for specific content areas and are used primarily for instructional purposes. Most often commercial texts have to be ordered directly from the publisher—you do not find them in bookstores or public libraries.

Trade books are books that we find in bookstores and libraries. They are sometimes called *authentic literature* because they are primarily written to communicate a message to the reader rather than for a specific program. Authors who write these books are most interested in conveying their ideas, and they do so using a variety of words and illustrations. For purposes of this book, we consider children's literature, authentic literature, and trade books to be the same.

The term *other books* is used to list texts that don't fit neatly into either of the previous two categories. Magazines and newspapers fall into this category.

Figure 3.1 lists the different texts that can be used for guided reading and the most appropriate grade levels in which they can be used. Following the figure is additional information about each type of text, including description, examples, references for more titles, why a teacher might want to use the text, and suggestions for guided reading. Regardless of the suggestions, keep in mind that what they all have in common is effective lesson design (see page 81). That is, each lesson is designed with the understanding that there are three parts to the reading lesson—*before*, *during*, and *after* reading—and that specific teaching strategies must be used at each phase to prepare children for a successful reading experience.

Two points of confusion can surface when we talk about using different texts in guided reading. One centers on how trade books are used in other programs. Sometimes the best of the trade books are selected for grade-level anthologies that, when taken together, comprise a reading program (i.e., basal readers). Another point of confusion centers on the idea of "leveled" books. Basically, these are collections of books from two categories—commercial *and* trade—that are separated according to difficulty. As Figure 3.2 (see page 32) shows, specific features are used to determine a book's level of difficulty. (For information about some of the problems associated with leveling books, see Peterson, 1991.)

Commercial Books
Little Books

Description   Little books are small books that can be easily held by young children. Usually, they are the same size, with a paperback cover and few pages. Many times, these books are written by different authors. All titles are then leveled by the company that produces them and are assembled into sets of readers that can be used for guided reading instruction.

Examples   Sets of little books are available from a number of publishers, including the following:

The Sunshine Series (Wright Group)

Literacy 2000 (Rigby)

Windows on Literacy (National Geographic)

People, Spaces, and Places (Rand McNally)

Text Type/Grade Level	1	2	3	4	5	6
Commercial Books						
Little books	•	•				
Basal readers	•	•	•	•	•	•
Textbooks	•	•	•	•	•	•
Children's Literature						
Predictable books	•	•				
Information (nonfiction)	•	•	•	•	•	•
Multilevel literature	•	•	•	•	•	•
Series books	•	•	•	•	•	•
Poetry	•	•	•	•	•	•
Chapter books		•	•	•	•	•
Multicultural literature	•	•	•	•	•	•
Other						
Newspapers	•	•	•	•	•	•
Magazines	•	•	•	•	•	•

FIGURE 3.1 Texts for guided reading

References for additional titles

Fountas, I., and Pinnell, G. S. 1999. *Matching Books to Readers: Using Leveled Books in Guided Reading, K–3.* Portsmouth, NH: Heinemann.

Gunning, T. 1998. *Best Books for Beginning Readers.* Boston: Allyn and Bacon.

Why use them?   Little books are designed especially for use with beginning readers, sometimes starting in kindergarten and continuing through first grade. They are often used with second-grade children as well. Because leveled texts are packaged in multiple sets, the books can be used for demonstrations and interventions with young readers in small-group settings. Likewise, the increasingly challenging texts facilitate the scaffolded instruction that was discussed earlier.

The sets of little books have the look and feel of real books and their use most closely parallels reading experiences in which children's literature is used. The books have a strong appeal to young readers because they convey a sense of reading whole books. Generally inexpensive, they can be used to create a classroom library of accessible books for use during independent reading time as well as guided reading.

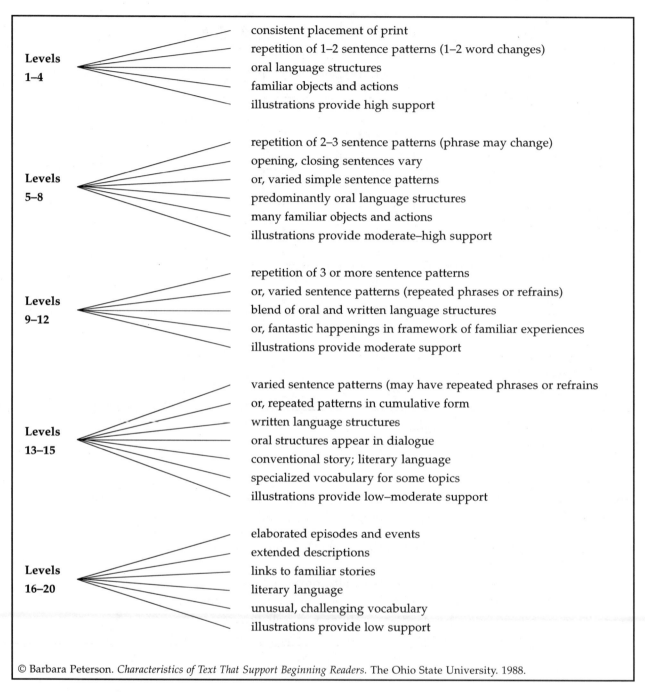

**Levels
1–4**
- consistent placement of print
- repetition of 1–2 sentence patterns (1–2 word changes)
- oral language structures
- familiar objects and actions
- illustrations provide high support

**Levels
5–8**
- repetition of 2–3 sentence patterns (phrase may change)
- opening, closing sentences vary
- or, varied simple sentence patterns
- predominantly oral language structures
- many familiar objects and actions
- illustrations provide moderate–high support

**Levels
9–12**
- repetition of 3 or more sentence patterns
- or, varied sentence patterns (repeated phrases or refrains)
- blend of oral and written language structures
- or, fantastic happenings in framework of familiar experiences
- illustrations provide moderate support

**Levels
13–15**
- varied sentence patterns (may have repeated phrases or refrains)
- or, repeated patterns in cumulative form
- written language structures
- oral structures appear in dialogue
- conventional story; literary language
- specialized vocabulary for some topics
- illustrations provide low–moderate support

**Levels
16–20**
- elaborated episodes and events
- extended descriptions
- links to familiar stories
- literary language
- unusual, challenging vocabulary
- illustrations provide low support

© Barbara Peterson. *Characteristics of Text That Support Beginning Readers.* The Ohio State University. 1988.

FIGURE 3.2 Text features

Suggestions for guided reading
- Select an appropriate title for a group of children who are reading at a similar general achievement level. After providing an introduction to the text, invite children to read it to themselves.

- After the children have read the book, engage them in one or more ways. They can discuss the text and read the part each liked the best.
- If focusing on teaching different ways to decipher unknown words, select a word from the text that posed difficulty, write it and the sentence in which it appears for all to see, and ask children how they can go about figuring out this unknown word.
- Using some common element, such as a story setting, select texts at different levels to represent the readers in the group. After children have had time to read their assigned books, teach students about story setting. Allow students time to share where their story took place.

Basal Readers

Description   Basal readers are the central components of commercially developed reading programs. They are often structured as anthologies of grade-leveled texts surrounded by a number of additional supportive materials such as teacher guides and student workbooks. Basal readers are usually selected and purchased to provide a cohesive, consistent, continuous reading curricula across and among grade levels throughout a school district or at individual schools. In most classrooms, each child is provided with a copy of the anthology (i.e., reader) to use during guided reading.

Examples   These are some of the most common basal readers:

Celebrate Literacy (1997, Scott Foresman)

Invitations to Literacy (1996, Houghton Mifflin)

Literacy Place (2000, Scholastic)

References for additional titles

Fawson, P., and D. Reutzel. 2000. "But I only have a basal: Implementing guided reading in the early grades." *The Reading Teacher* 54(1): 84–97.

McCarthy, S., and J. Hoffman. 1995. "The new basals: How are they different?" *The Reading Teacher* 49(1): 72–75.

Why use them?   The use of basal readers is very much encouraged and expected in many school districts. In fact, after readers are purchased, little if any money is left to buy other materials that could be used to teach reading. One reason for using basal readers, then, has to do with district level expectations; another has to do with access. All students are provided with books and teachers are provided with materials for instructional support.

For the most part, the selections in readers are organized by increasingly sophisticated vocabulary, concepts, and text structures. Thus, the selections within the anthologies can be used to scaffold instruction in much the same way as little books are.

Suggestions for guided reading

- Choose individual selections within a basal reader to use for a demonstration or intervention (see Chapter 2).

- Newer basal reading anthologies have the added advantage of having selections organized by theme. Using these themed stories for common and shared response activities with small groups of students is natural. Students can be assigned to read the same selection within a theme and then share something of interest. Another way to capitalize on the use of themed stories is to have different students read different stories within the same theme. Once finished, students can compare and contrast their stories.

Textbooks

Description   Besides the materials purchased for and used in the classroom reading/language arts program, a number of other commercially prepared texts are written to be used to instruct in specific content areas (e.g., science, social studies, and mathematics). Often, one series is selected for a whole school district or specific school. A series is most often comprised of a set of common core texts each containing grade-level-appropriate presentations of increasingly sophisticated subject area content. Each student is provided a copy of the grade-level text.

Examples   Scholastic, Prentice-Hall, and Silver/Burdett/Ginn are the publishers of some of the most widely used textbooks.

Why use them?   Both teachers and students should have easy access to these materials. They are often selected, purchased, and distributed as a foundation for content area curricula. Like basal readers, the use of textbooks is strongly encouraged because often a wealth of resources has been used to purchase them. Therefore, a good reason to use textbooks is to meet externally mandated expectations. Another, perhaps more essential, reason for using textbooks focuses on student success. As we all know, students encounter textbook-based instruction in specific content areas, and students' success can depend on their ability to handle the reading demands of these texts. Because they differ from other more storylike selections, then, using textbooks for guided reading instruction is one way to expose students to them. The goal is to improve their ability to negotiate their way through textbooks with maximum comprehension.

Suggestions for guided reading

- Choose a specific section of a textbook and show students how to do a preview as a warm-up for successful reading. After students have previewed, allow time for them to read the text to themselves. Once finished reading, have students relate information that they discovered.

- Most textbook chapters are divided by subheadings. Either assign or invite students to choose the section they would like to read and tell them to look for three specific ideas they can share with others in the group. After reading their section, have students in the group create a note-taking guide to record information about the sections of the chapter that they have not read yet.

Children's Literature
Predictable Books
Description   Predictable books are books written with specific features that enable children to read with ease. These characteristics are as follows:

- *Pictures that support the text*—The pictures show what the text says, making it possible for readers to use them to help read the text.
- *Repeated sentence or phrase*—The same sentence or phrase is repeated on nearly every page. The repetition helps young readers use memory to read the sentence or phrase.
- *Rhyme and rhythm*—The use of both enables the reader to use these language features to read the text.
- *Cumulative pattern*—As the story progresses, new lines are added but previous lines are repeated, providing the reader with practice.
- *Familiar sequence*—Days of the week or counting are two examples of this feature. Students use what they know about both to successfully read the text at hand.

Examples   Some examples of predictable books are:
   I Went Walking (Williams, 1990)

   The Jacket I Wear in the Snow (Neitzel, 1989)

   Polar Bear, Polar Bear, What Do You Hear? (Martin, 1991)

References for additional titles
Gunning, T. 1998. *Best Books for Beginning Readers*. Boston: Allyn and Bacon.

Opitz, M. 1995. *Getting the Most from Predictable Books*. New York: Scholastic.

Thogmartin, M. B. 1998. *Teach a Child to Read with Children's Books*, 2d ed. Bloomington, IN: Educational Resources Information Center.

Why use them?   Predictable books are advantageous for several reasons (see Opitz, 1995; Thogmartin, 1998 for detailed explanations). First, these books employ the language features just listed to enable children to read with greater ease. Second, predictable books enable children to read authentic literature from the very beginning, which helps them see that they can read "real" books. Third, although they are most often used with beginning readers, predictable books provide a tremendous amount of support and lead to success with reading for those whose first language is not English and for older children who struggle to read.

Suggestions for guided reading
- Select an appropriate title for a group of children who are reading at a similar achievement level. After providing an introduction to the text, invite children to read it to themselves.

- After they have read the book, engage the children in one or more ways. They may first discuss the text and then read the part that was liked the best.

- If focusing on teaching different ways to solve unknown words, select a word from the text that posed difficulty, write it and the sentence in which it appears for all to see, and ask children how they can go about figuring out this unknown word.

- Using some common element, such as a story setting, select texts at different levels to represent the readers in the group. After children have had time to read their assigned books, teach students about story setting. Allow students time to share where their story took place.

Information Books (Nonfiction)

Description   Nonfiction books are those that present factual information about a given topic. They are usually accompanied by photographs and illustrations to help students better understand the content.

Some examples of nonfictional information books:
   Animals in Disguise (Ganeri, 1995)

   Autumn: An Alphabet Acrostic (Schnur, 1997)

   Work (Morris, 1998)

References for additional titles
Bamford, R., and J. Kristo. 1998. *Making Facts Come Alive: Choosing Quality Nonfiction Literature, K–8*. Norwood, MA: Christopher-Gordon.

Donoghue, M. 2001. *Using Literature Activities to Teach Content Areas to Emergent Readers*. Boston: Allyn and Bacon.

Harvey, S. 1998. *Nonfiction Matters: Reading, Writing, and Research in Grades 3–8*. York, ME: Stenhouse.

Kobrin, B. 1995. *Eyeopeners II: Children's Books to Answer Children's Questions About the World Around Them*. New York: Scholastic.

Why use them?   There are two sound reasons for using information texts. First, they present information about the world around us. Because many children are curious about their surroundings, these texts provide motivating and interesting reading material. Second, the structures used to write information texts differ from those that are used to write fiction. To become competent readers, students need to learn how to read all of the different types of texts. Additional reasons are listed in the references just cited.

Suggestions for guided reading
- Select a text with specific features that you want to teach students. For example, you might want to show them how to read a diagram and how it relates to the written text. After providing instruction, have children read the text and follow up with a discussion in which they talk about how the diagram helped them read the text.

- Use a specific nonfiction selection to show students how to process the information presented: reading picture captions, subheadings, bold print, and so on. After providing this introduction, have students read the text. They can then report one or two ideas they learned from the text.

Multilevel Books
Description   Multilevel books are books that are written with multiple story lines. Books that have simple story lines and contain more information about specific features in the text at the end of the book are also considered multilevel. While some of these books are fiction, the majority are nonfiction (informational). Still others combine fiction and nonfiction.

Examples
> *Counting on Calico* (Tildes, 1995) is one nonfiction book that has two story lines.

> *Into the A, B, Sea* (Rose, 2000) is a nonfiction text that has a simple story line with accompanying information about each animal and plant at the back of the book.

> *Calico Picks a Puppy* (Tildes, 1996) is a multilevel book that contains three story lines.

> *Animals in Camouflage* (Tildes, 2000) is an example of a book that contains two story lines and information at the end of the text.

References for additional titles   Although there are no published references that highlight these texts, Appendix B contains a list of multilevel books. In addition to bibliographic information, the list provides a range of appropriate grade levels.

Why use them?   Regardless of reading level or background, all children can read some or all portions of this type of book. Using these texts, then, is one way of showing students that they can all read similar texts and get something out of the experience. Regardless of where they begin, all children are part of one community of learners.

The multilevel books are rich in content; they contain information about objects that are of great interest to children. As discussed before, the books expose children to reading an information text and also provide for meaningful repeated reading. Once children hear parts of the story from either the teacher or classmates, which is a form of scaffolding, they are more likely to be able to read the text themselves. Finally, in terms of a resource issue, more mileage can be "covered" with fewer dollars being spent.

Suggestions for guided reading

- If students are grouped by similar level or background, different groups can read different parts of the text. For example, those who are just getting a handle on how print functions or those who have little background about the topic at hand could be invited to follow along as the teacher reads a given part of the text. Once this has been accomplished, the teacher can have students choral read their part while he or she reads the additional text on the page, thus building children's background and knowledge base.

- Once each group member has read through the text focusing on the parts most appropriate for the given group, children can be grouped by twos (if the book has two story lines or parts) or threes (if the book has three story lines or parts). In turn, each person can read his or her part of the text while others listen. To emphasize listening comprehension, each group could be given one text that is passed from one person to the next as each part has been read.

- If in pairs and the focus is on helping the inexperienced reader attain a larger reading vocabulary, plus hear an example of fluent reading, each child can be given a copy of the text. Then the less-experienced reader can follow along as the partner reads aloud. This particular way of reading provides the less-experienced reader—or one with limited background—with a scaffold, thus ensuring that this child too will be able to read a good portion of the text in the near future.

Series Books

Description   Series books are those that share common elements such as characters, author's style, words, and format. Children can often follow the development of story's characters and share in their adventures in each succeeding book in the series.

Examples   Some well-known series books are:

Claudia Mills, *Gus and Grandpa* (grades 1–2)

Patricia Reilly-Giff, *Polk Street Kids* (grades 2–3)

Dan Greenburg, *Zack Files* (grades 2–5)

J. K. Rowling, *Harry Potter* (grades 4–6)

References for additional titles

Conversations (Routman, 2000)—Pages 76b through 78b provide series
books according to those that are most appealing to children in given
grade levels. They are divided into the following categories: Easy
Reader Format (grades 1–2), Easy Chapter Book Series (grades 2–3),
Transitional Series Books (grades 2–5), and those in a more challenging
series for older readers (grades 4–7).

Richeck, M. A., and B. K. McTague. 1988. The "Curious George" strategy
for students with reading problems. *The Reading Teacher* 42: 220–26.

Worthy, J. 1996. "A matter of interest: Literature that hooks reluctant
readers and keeps them reading." *The Reading Teacher* 50(3): 204–12.

Why use them?   Series books can be a very effective source of reading
material for three reasons. First, they provide meaningful reading practice.
Once children get hooked, they have a desire to read other books in the
series. Because characters, plot structure, and words are common to all
books in the series, students are provided with a lot of meaningful practice.
In other words, the natural redundancy of these features provides support
for the most novice of readers, enabling children to read these texts more
easily. Much confidence results!

Second, the series books provide opportunities for children to discuss
and interpret events. Students reading different or like titles in the series
often make their own interpretations based on their backgrounds. Talking
with others broadens understanding.

Third, they provide children with opportunities to make inferences.
When reading the books out of order, especially, children must infer what
has come before and how their book fits into the series. In effect, as they
read different books in the series, children get to solve a reading puzzle.
Solving this puzzle can be very engaging for students and is even more
challenging when the books in the series are numbered yet are read out of
order.

Suggestions for guided reading

■   Group students according to those reading the same series. Children
can then discuss their books with teacher guidance. Several different
teaching points could emerge. For example, what all of the books have

in common might be a focal point. Another might be to discuss how reading series books can increase comprehension.

- To help children experience being a part of a larger community of readers, provide each child in the class with a different book in the series. Children can then be grouped in a variety of ways for guided reading instruction. For example, those children who need to learn how to better use words to create visual images can be grouped together to learn how to do so. Those children who need to learn how to pay attention to meaning as well as visual cues can be grouped together. After they have been taught the given strategy, they can then practice it using their series book while the teacher provides guidance.

Poetry

Description   Poetry is writing in which rhythm, sound, and language are used to create images, thoughts, and emotional responses. Usually concise, poetry takes on many forms—*narrative poetry* tells a story, *lyric poetry* uses a lot of rhythm, *humorous poetry* portrays everyday objects or events in absurd ways, and *nonsense poetry* uses meaningless words and much exaggeration (Goforth, 1998).

Examples   The following are three examples of poetry books:

If You're Not Here, Please Raise Your Hand: Poems About School (Dakos, 1995)

Joyful Noise: Poems for Two Voices (Fleischman, 1989)

On the Wing (Florian, 1996)

References for additional titles:
Goforth, F. 1998. *Literature and the Learner*. Belmont, CA: Wadsworth.
Heard, G. 1998. *Awakening the Heart: Exploring Poetry in Elementary and Middle School*. Portsmouth, NH: Heinemann.
Sweeney, J. 1993. *Teaching Poetry: Yes, You Can!* New York: Scholastic.

Why use it?   As with other forms of writing, poetry is written using different formats. Exposing children to this form of writing, then, opens up this style of writing to them, making their comprehension of it more likely. Because many poems are succinct and are written with words that convey images, poems are excellent to use to help children learn to visualize. Likewise, because they are short, poems tend to be less intimidating for even the most novice reader. Finally, poetry helps students develop numerous reading skills, including phrasing, fluency, and comprehension.

Suggestions for guided reading

■ Select a given poem to help students learn how to use words from it to create visual images. After modeling the process, provide students with another poem, and allow time for them to read it. Once read, have students discuss specific lines and the images they saw when they read it.

■ To model fluency and reading poetry for enjoyment, select a poem and read it to the students. Point out how the phrases helped you know how to read the poem. Next, provide students with several poetry books. Invite them to choose one book, then identify and read a poem. Once read, have students read their poems aloud to the group.

■ Students can also create materials to use during guided reading experiences after they become familiar with some core poems you introduce during shared reading. Lines or stanzas from the poems can be printed on one side of a blank page. During independent work time, students can add illustrations and bind the pages to create their own text. The teacher can then invite them to bring their book to the guided reading table to use for demonstration and intervention lessons.

Chapter Books

Description   Chapter books are books that are broken into different segments or chapters. They range in sophistication, beginning with the very easiest in first grade. Chapter books increase in difficulty throughout the grades.

Examples

■ chapter books for younger readers:

  The *Henry and Mudge* series by Cynthia Rylant

  The *Frog and Toad* series by Arnold Lobel

■ chapter books for older readers:

  Recent Newbery award and honor books

  Bud, Not Buddy by Christopher Curtis

  Missing May by Cynthia Rylant

  The Giver by Lois Lowry

  Walk Two Moons by Sharon Creech

  Shiloh by Phyliss Naylor

References for additional titles
Buss, K. and L. Karnowski. 2000. *Reading and Writing Literary Genres*.
    Newark, DE: International Reading Association.

Children's Choices. 1995. *More Kids' Favorite Books*. Newark, DE: International Reading Association.

Hearn, B. 1990. *Choosing Books for Children: A Commonsense Guide*. New
    York: Delacorte.

Why use them?   Chapter books afford children an opportunity to extend themselves into books that they will be reading in their everyday lives. These books help students learn how a story is connected by use of individual chapters. They also signal to children that they are becoming more competent readers. For instructional purposes, chapter books also easily provide logical stopping points.

Cynthia Rylant, Patricia Reilly-Giff, Gary Paulsen, and William Steig are a few authors who have written at all levels—picture books, simple chapter books, complex young adult novels, and adult fiction and nonfiction. Studying these authors will allow teachers with a wide range of readers in their classroom to match appropriate texts to student's levels while still engaging them in a cohesive, classroom conversation about an author.

Suggestions for guided reading
- Provide all students in the group with the same chapter book and provide a structure for reading the book.

- Use chapter books to engage children in an author study. Different groups of children can read different chapter books by the same author. Author style across texts can become a focal point for instruction.

Multicultural Books
Description   Multicultural literature refers to all genres that portray the likenesses and differences among social, cultural, and ethnic groups. They are written to reflect our diverse society.

Examples   The following are three useful multicultural books:
The Serpent's Tongue: Prose, Poetry, and Art of the New Mexico Pueblos (Wood, 1997; grades 5–6)

When Jessie Came Across the Sea (Hest, 1997; grades 1–6)

America: My Land, Your Land, Our Land (Nikoli-Lisa, 1997; grades 1–2)

References for additional titles
Barrera, R., V. Thompson, and M. Dressman. 1997. *Kaleidoscope*, 2d ed.
    Urbana, IL: National Council of Teachers of English.

Harris, V., ed. 1997. *Using Multicultural Literature in the K–8 Classroom.* Norwood, MA: Christopher-Gordon.

Why use it?   All children need books that represent their cultural heritage. In this way they can have characters with whom to identify. Multicultural literature also provides children with opportunities to learn about the similarities among and differences among people and to consider different points of view.

Suggestions for guided reading
- Select a topic or theme on which to focus that will encourage students to select multicultural books during guided reading instruction. For example, if the focus was on the impact of prejudice and discrimination, students can explore nonfiction and fiction titles at many different levels. Some might be reading picture books, such as Robert Coles' *Ruby Bridges,* and others might be reading novellas, such as Mildred Taylor's *The Gold Cadillac.* You then bring groups of students together to discuss the issues and ideas in their books that relate to the topic.

- Encourage critical literacy by selecting certain texts and then guiding students in looking at those texts from perspectives other than their own. When working on a frontier/pioneer theme, you may have small groups of students reading different trade books such as Laura Ingalls Wilder's *Little House in the Big Woods* and Carolyn Brink's *Caddie Woodlawn.* You can stucture certain discussions so that students respond to what was written by assuming roles (Native Americans, pioneer children, modern women, and so on). Assuming different perspectives will help readers critically analyze texts that you are reading. Introducing contrasting texts—such as Michael Dorris' *Sees Behind Trees,* which is written from a Native American perspective— allows the teacher to guide students through additional comparisons and contrasts by looking critically at historical events.

Other Texts
Magazines
Description   Magazines are compilations of articles and stories designed to inform readers about many different topics. Columns of text, pictures with captions, short tidbits about different topics, diagrams, and advertisements are used often to create a magazine. Most magazines focus on a specific audience and feature articles that would appeal to this audience.

Examples   Some of the best-known children's magazines are:
Sesame Street Magazine (ages 0–6)

Zoobooks (ages 6–14)

Cricket Magazine (ages 8–14)

Reference for additional titles
Stoll, D., ed. 1997. *Magazines for Kids and Teens, Revised ed.* Glassboro, NJ: Educational Press Association of America; Newark, DE: International Reading Association.

Why use them?   Reading a magazine requires the reader to be magazine literate. According to Stoll (1997), being *magazine literate* means that the reader knows how the publication works—its organization, where to locate specific information, and how to maximize the potential of the magazine. Using magazines for guided reading, then, is an excellent way to help students become magazine literate. Time can be devoted to teaching children how to read them and that magazines reflect many different personalities.

Because some contain articles written by children and high-interest articles, magazines also provide very motivating reading material. They can serve as a catalyst for meaningful writing experiences too; students can be encouraged to write their own articles for publication and to write letters to the editor. Finally, because columns of text, pictures with short captions, short blurbs about given topics, and diagrams are used in magazines, a lot of information can be accessed by all readers.

Suggestions for guided reading
- Choose a specific magazine and design a guided reading experience to show students its features: how it's organized, the table of contents, the variety of articles, and so on. Students could then choose an article to read and share what they discover with the rest of the group.

- Some magazines, such as *Zoobooks,* devote an entire issue to a given topic (e.g., elephants). Provide a copy of the magazine for each student in the group. Show them how to skim the text looking for facts about elephants. Then, have students do the same, this time looking for at least three facts about elephants that they want to share with others. As they report, make a chart that shows what they've found.

Newspapers
Description: Newspapers are collections of informational articles, advertisements, comics, and so on, which are put together to inform the public of current events. Most are published daily although some that are written specifically for classroom use are published weekly.

Examples   The most useful newspapers for teaching purposes are the following:

Weekly Reader (preschool–grade 6)

Scholastic News (grades 1–6)

kids' page or mini page from a local newspaper (grades 1–3)

and any local newspaper (grades 3–6)

References for additional titles

Olivares, R. 1993. *Using the Newspaper to Teach ESL Learners.* Newark, DE: International Reading Association.

Stoll, D., ed. 1997. *Magazines for Kids and Teens, Revised ed.* Glassboro, NJ: Educational Press Association of America; Newark, DE: International Reading Association.

Why use them?   Newspapers provide a wealth of reading material about everyday life. They have current events information at several levels. Like other reading materials, however, they are written with a specific format. Readers must learn how news articles are written so that they can get the information they need and successfully negotiate their way through the paper without feeling overwhelmed. Guided reading is a perfect fit! Specific newspapers and articles within newspapers can be used to show students the variety of texts newspapers use and how to read each one.

Students can also be shown how to read articles so that they are looking for the answers to questions that most articles address: who, what, when, where, why, and how. Using newspapers also helps students increase their knowledge of the world and given topics, thus enhancing their reading comprehension of these same topics when they are encountered in other texts. Finally, using newspapers helps students to see themselves as "real-life" readers. They see others reading newspapers outside of school and begin to recognize that they can do the same.

Suggestions for guided reading

- Use the mini-page of the local newspaper to show students how the newspaper is organized. If the purpose of using the newspaper is to show students that articles focus on specific questions (who, what, when, where, why), list these key words on the board and direct students to read a specific article looking for answers to these questions.

- As with other texts, news stories can present some challenging words for students to decipher. You may want to show students how to use context clues to determine the meaning of unknown words. Once modeled, have students apply this strategy to an article they choose to read or one that you have chosen for them.

How Do We Know Which Text to Use at Any Given Time?

Choosing texts for a guided reading experience takes quite a bit of thought. It is anything but a haphazard guess, as Gates (1928) acknowledged more than seventy years ago. In his words, "In the first place, the use of a wide variety of reading materials and purposes has not been the result of chance but the outcome of a definite plan to develop various important phases of reading" (p. 225).

Sometimes what makes text selection difficult are the different views about the types of texts that children should be reading during guided reading. Recently, for example, some are advocating that children who are just learning to read should be reading "decodable" text (i.e., text which is constructed by using specific letter–sound patterns). High-frequency words are also used. Providing these texts, advocates claim, provides children who are just beginning to read with opportunities to apply phonics skills and learn a store of sight words at the same time (Brown, 1999/2000; Mesmer, 1999).

Although this may be true, there is little evidence that it is so. As Cunningham (2000) states:

> There is research evidence to support providing children with lots of "readable text"—text they can read easily. But there are no studies that suggest children learn to read better when the text they are reading is restricted to only those words they have been taught to decode (p. 183).

In fact, these texts may cause more problems than they solve (Gill, 2000). As Teale and Yokota (2000) note, the language used in the text is distorted and the stories are often uninteresting, leading children away from reading rather than inviting them to it. Others agree that decodable texts are not storybooks (Pearson, 1999; Routman, 2000).

So what's a teacher to do? When selecting texts for your students, we suggest considering three key variables simultaneously: the purpose of your instruction, the students with whom you are working, and the texts to which you have access. We suggest that you use the following guidelines.

Determine the Purpose for the Guided Reading Experience

Determining the specific strategies you are trying to help students learn is what will assist you in choosing the appropriate text(s) to use. In other words, different types of texts elicit different comprehension strategies. Say, for example, you want to teach students how to identify clues that can be used to draw conclusions. Using mysteries would enable you to accomplish this purpose. On the other hand, perhaps your goal is to help students learn how to follow printed instructions. In this case, you would most likely choose procedural text, often featured in a magazine or newspaper—one in which students need to follow specific steps in order to successfully complete a task.

Think About Your Students

What we want during a guided reading experience are texts that children can read with some assistance. We want the books to be within their "instructional range"—reading with 91 to 94 percent word accuracy and 60 to 75 percent comprehension. There are at least four ways that we can ensure this:

■ One way to determine instructional level is to assess students both on word accuracy and comprehension. When these two scores do not match, and they often do not, we suggest that you focus on the comprehension score first. That is, choose material in which the child is demonstrating adequate comprehension. As discussed earlier, remember that instructional range can and does change depending on several factors. A child might very well be reading a book that we consider well beyond his or her "level" one day and the next day struggle with an "on-level" book. This is so because many factors contribute to the successful reading of a text (see Chapter 1 for a review of these factors). Therefore, other factors, such as student interest and background, are as important as instructional range.

■ Adjust teaching strategies so that the book can be brought within the child's instructional range; there are several ways this can be accomplished. If, for example, you know the child may be struggling because of limited background, you can spend more time at the beginning phase of the reading experience to build background. If, on the other hand, the material will be a challenge because the child may be overwhelmed with the amount of text, you can break it up in different ways and have children read different parts. If lack of interest is the issue, you can generate interest by connecting the reading experience to something of interest in the students' lives. The scenarios shown in Chapter Four provide concrete examples.

■ Alter the way the text is introduced. Should it be needed, we can provide a very rich introduction; in effect, the text is all but read to the child. We can also provide less of an introduction if we feel the students need less. The goal with these introductions is to set the children up for a successful reading experience yet one in which they can "work" the text (Clay, 1991b; Watson, 1997).

■ Allow for student choice. All of us are more likely to read a text—even if it may be considered beyond us—if we are interested in it. So it is with children. Yes, we will have to dismiss the "instructional level" in its truest sense. According to the children, however, the text is still within the "instructional range" because they have an inner desire to read it. Then, too, we know that the text itself can serve as a learning tool (Alexander & Jetton, 2000; Goldman & Rakestraw, 2000). Will they need more support to help them realize their goal? Without a doubt! How fortunate for us that we get to provide it.

Consider Your Resources

You may be teaching in a school that has a rich resource of books. You also may be teaching in one that is just the opposite. Considering your students and your resources may help you decide which texts to use. For example, if you want to integrate reading with social studies, you may decide to use a text set that deals with relationships. You have very few books at your disposal, so you decide to visit your school library and the local library in search of some titles. You discover several titles that would work, each written at different levels of complexity. To select the books, you think about your students and settle on five or six titles that you will use during your guided reading lesson. Each of the books will be best-suited to the different students' reading levels. Once back in the room, you group the children into mixed-achievement groups so that every child will be able to read one book when they read with you during guided reading.

On the other hand, let's say that your school has a rich resource of books. In fact, your school has a guided reading room in which collections of books are kept in baskets according to levels and/or topics. When you want specific books, you go to the room and select them. Now you have a couple of options. Assuming that you still want to integrate reading and social studies by focusing on relationships, you go to the room in search of books at different levels that relate to the topic. You discover four titles that have something to do with relationships.

Once back in the room, you make the decision to group the children by like title; all those that can read a given level with relative ease and with adequate comprehension are grouped together. However, recognizing that students can learn from one another, you also decide that once each group has read its title, you will also group the students by different titles so that each group member has a different title for one or two days. On the first day, students "book talk" their books and share something from the text that they are prepared to read. The next day, students talk about what their books have in common. They can also swap books and read alone or with a partner.

Remember That There Is No One Formula

There are several types of texts that can be used during guided reading. However, there is no ready formula that provides you with the perfect mix of texts that you should use. What we *do know* is that children must be exposed to a variety of texts if they are to become accomplished readers!

CHAPTER FOUR

Instruction

The previous chapters focused attention on the considerations for successful guided reading experiences. The purpose of this chapter is to combine these pieces to give you a sense of how they all work together. We "drop in" on the classroom instruction of nine teachers as they implement a variety of guided reading experiences at different grade levels. Each classroom scenario starts with the four main considerations that need to be addressed before planning purposeful guided reading experiences (see Figure 4.1):

- What is my purpose?
- How should I organize my groups?
- What texts should I use?
- Should I select the texts or should students select them?

Addressing these considerations beforehand will make reading success more likely for students during guided reading instruction. You will also need to determine how much time you need to conduct the lesson.

Purpose for the Guided Reading Experience	Grouping Technique		Text Considerations			Text Selection	
	Similar Achievement	Mixed Achievement	Single Titles	Multiple Titles	Leveled Titles	Student	Teacher
Demonstration							
Strategy	•	•	•	•	•		•
Literary element		•		•		•	•
Procedures	•	•	•				•
Intervention							
Single need	•		•		•		•
Multiple need		•		•	•	•	•
Shared response							
Single	•	•	•			•	•
Multiple		•		•		•	•
Combination	•	•	•	•	•	•	•

FIGURE 4.1 Considerations for purposeful guided reading experiences

How Does Guided Reading Play Out in Different Classrooms?

To show you some of the ways that these considerations are addressed by different teachers, we offer scenarios from different grade levels. The majority of the scenarios show that small-group guided reading experiences are often an outgrowth of reading instruction conducted with the entire class. Guided reading is used to provide children with additional support and practice. As Figure 4.2 shows, the scenarios occur for different lengths of time; some happen within one day, others span anywhere from two to five days. As you read through these scenarios, keep in mind that they are offered here as suggestions of the many possibilities associated with guided reading; there are many different combinations of these variables that can be used.

Use the information in these scenarios as a starting point to imagine and design your own possibilities! Doing so will enable you to create a flexible, fluid system that you can adjust easily to respond to the unique needs of your students. Also, keep in mind that in all of the scenarios teachers have already established the routines and procedures for effective guided reading instruction such as those presented in Chapter 5.

Scenario	Page	Grade	Day(s)	Time
1	50	Paul's First Grade	1	20 min.
2	52	Abby's First Grade	1	20 min.
3	57	Juliet's Second Grade	2–3	30 min.
4	59	Danette's Third Grade	2	20 min.
5	61	Chuck's Fourth Grade	2	45–60 min.
6	63	Mac's Fifth Grade	2	60 min.
7	68	Patti's Fifth Grade	5	45 min.
8	73	Joe's Sixth Grade	1	45 min.
9	75	Kerry's Sixth Grade	5	45 min.

FIGURE 4.2 Overview of scenarios

Scenario 1: Paul's First Grade

About the Scenario

Past lessons have shown Paul that small-group guided reading instruction is a natural extension of large-group instruction. In this scenario, Paul shows how he moves from large-group to small-group instruction to provide children with the necessary support to read a text.

Before the Guided Reading Experience

Paul uses the big book *Mr. Grump* (Cowley, 1989) during a shared reading experience conducted with the whole class. During this time, he observes that some readers seem to need additional instruction to strengthen their concepts print—noticing print on the page, directionality, voice–print match. He decides to group these students together to provide this instruction. Paul has also thought through the following considerations.

1. *Purpose:* A combination—demonstration (concept of prints strategies), intervention (concepts of print), and shared response
2. *Grouping technique:* Similar achievement level small group (emergent readers)
3. *Text considerations:* Single text (multiple copies)
4. *Text selection:* Teacher
5. *Time:* 20 minutes

During the Guided Reading Experience

Paul secures multiple copies of little book versions of *Mr. Grump* and invites six students to join him on the carpet for a guided reading experience. He sits in the middle of a semicircle within arm reach of all students. By sitting in the middle of the group as opposed to across from them, all students will be able to see the big book without looking at it upside down. He begins with the big-book version, saying, "Yesterday we read this in the whole group. Let's go back through the book so that we can better remember what happened in the story." He opens to the first page, saying, "Look what we have here! We have both pictures and words on this page *(pointing to each)*. When I read, I have to make sure that I am looking at the words. I can use the pictures to help me with some of the words but to be reading, I have to be looking at the words because it's the words that tell the story."

As a demonstration using a small pointer, Paul rereads the story. He also tells his students that readers start at the top of the page and on the left side. He points to where he will start. Then he reminds the students that he will say each of the words on the page. He starts reading the words carefully, pointing to each one, and matching his voice to the words. When he gets to the end of a line, Paul shows his students how he needs to start again on the left side by modeling the return sweep. As he turns each page, he starts the modeling over again, reminding the students to start at the top and on the left side before saying each word as he touches it. His students' increasing familiarity with the story causes them to join in on repeated phrases in the story during the rereading.

After he finishes his demonstration, Paul comments, "You've just seen me read the story. Now it's your turn." He distributes the books and reminds the readers to leave the books flat on the carpet in front of him so that he can see how everyone is reading. He then invites the students to turn to the beginning of the story. Paul asks the students to tell him where the words are and where the story starts. He tells each student to put his or her finger on the first word in the story. Again, he models using the big book, which all students can see. He encourages the students to try to touch each word as they say them. He carefully guides the reading of the page by leading the students through the text. With each page, he tells the students to show where the words are, where the story starts, and to put their finger on the first word of each page.

Using an observation grid, Paul notes which students seem to be responding or not responding accurately to his questions and directives. As a way of furthering their understanding of the concepts of print and to judge the level of their independent behaviors, he decides to call on some individual students to model for the others.

Following the Guided Reading Experience

After the intervention, Paul provides the students with a few minutes to respond to the text. He passes out two index cards to each student. He asks them to write "yes" on one card and "no" on the other card; he models this for them. Then he asks three questions about the story for them to respond to: Do you know someone like Mr. Grump? Have you ever felt like Mr. Grump? Does Mr. Grump remind you of a character in any other story we have read? Students flash their yes/no cards in response to each question, and Paul follows up with individual students based on those responses. After a brief discussion about the story, he pairs up students and invites them to practice reading together as he observes.

Before using the same text with another group of students for a more sophisticated lesson on word identification strategies, Paul quickly reviews his notes and reflects on how the children performed. This reflection helps him to remember which students need additional support with the print concepts in future guided reading experiences and which students appear to be ready for additional skills and strategies.

Scenario 2: Abby's First Grade

About the Scenario

Abby is a first-grade teacher who realizes the importance of using guided reading. To ensure her success as well as her students', she has attended to several organizational features before they arrive for the first day of school (see Chapter 5 for additional information). She has leveled all of the little books she has and placed them in clearly identified baskets—each basket is labeled with a different letter of the alphabet. Abby has also prepared guided reading folders. Students will keep the book they are currently reading in their folder along with an individual reading record on which students will record the books they have read.

She has also prepared a three-ring notebook that contains a tabbed section for each student; Abby will use this to record information while working with students. At the back of this notebook, she has several matrices that have space to write the students' names down the left side and information categories across the top. She will use these grids to record her observations as she assists students.

The scenario here takes place the second month of school. Abby has explained the guided reading procedures to students and each understands how to use the guided reading folder.

Before the Guided Reading Experience

Classroom observations have enabled Abby to see that her twenty-five first graders have diverse literacy needs. Nine of the students have similar needs, and she has decided to teach these students in a guided reading group. She has thoughtfully considered the following elements to get most from this guided reading instruction.

1. *Purpose:* Intervention (differentiated based individuals' miscues; word identification strategies)
2. *Grouping technique:* Similar achievement small-group instruction
3. *Text considerations:* A variety of little-book titles within a restricted range of levels; some are familiar to readers and others are unfamiliar
4. *Text selection:* Readers choose the texts from Abby's preselected collection of titles that represent different levels
5. *Time:* 20 minutes

During the Guided Reading Experience

Abby calls the nine students to the carpeted area. She invites them to practice with the titles in their folders for the first few minutes of the group time. The students take out their books and begin reading. While students engage in this independent reading, Abby listens to one child read orally and takes a running record. A glance through her notebook reminds her that she needs to read with Carl, who is reading *In the Mirror*. After five or so minutes—enough time for the students to practice their titles to warm up their reading and for her to complete Carl's running record—Abby gathers the students together near her on the carpet. A quick analysis of the running record shows that Carl had difficulty pronouncing four words: *fingers, nose, knee,* and *monster*. She will use these words to help students better understand how they can figure out both the pronunciation and the meaning of unknown words.

She begins by having students put their books back into their folders so that they can all focus on Carl's book. Abby takes his book and shows them the page that contains the word "fingers." Pointing to the word, she asks group members to think about how they would figure out how to say this word and how they would figure out if it makes sense in the story. She systematically calls on Carl first, who suggests that they could chunk the word. Picking up on his idea, Abby writes "fingers" on the small white board for all to see.

When Carl has difficulty chunking the word, she quickly moves to the student sitting next to him in the circle. She asks Sean to take over. He chunks the word by identifying *fing, ers* and putting them together to say the word "fingers." Abby then asks Sean to continue and to explain how he can check to see if he is right. Sean says he knows he's right because the pictures show some fingers. Abby notes his comments as well as Carl's on her word identification strategy grid.

Abby proceeds in a like manner with the rest of the words, moving systematically around the circle and making sure all students have an opportunity to share and demonstrate the strategies they would use to learn the pronunciation and the meaning of words they may not know. You can get a good sense of how Abby interacts with her students by reviewing the transcript in Figure 4.3.

She also notes their ideas for solving unknown words so that she can add them to a chart—Ways to Figure Out Words—which she displays in the classroom for all to see. She invites students to add to this list to create an excellent reference for everyone in the classroom. On a day when Abby has more time, she will invite a second student to read his or her book. She will quickly make a running record on that child's reading and use the miscues to continue the intervention on word identification strategies.

After the Guided Reading Experience

As she dismisses the students, she reminds them that they can practice reading their books any time during the day. She also reminds them that they can take their books home to share with their families if they can read them without running into any difficulties.

Abby reflects on the lesson so that she can determine what to do tomorrow. She reviews the notes she took during the lesson using the group grid for miscue analysis (see Figure 4.4). She noted the following information for each student:

1. What word did the student try to identify?
2. How did the student identify it?
3. Could the student identify and use an effective strategy?
4. Could the student cross-check with a second strategy?

T:	Let's see if we can figure out this word. *[Shows page with FINGERS on it]* Carl, how could we figure out this word?
Carl:	Chunking.
T:	*[Writes FINGERS on white board]* Do you see a chunk you know?
Carl:	*[Shrugs Shoulders]*
T:	Sean, can you try that strategy and see what you get?
Sean:	ING—FING—ERS . . . FINGERS. . . .
T:	How can we tell if FINGERS is right?
Sean:	You can tell by the picture.
T:	Let's see if we can figure out this word. *[Shows page with NOSE on it]* Kyle, what strategy could we use?
Kyle:	N—O—S . . . NOS
T:	How are you trying to figure it out?
Kyle:	*[No response]*
T:	Reid, what could we do to figure it out?
Reid:	Look at the picture—NOSE.
T:	Let's check to see if that works. Can you reread that page, Reid?
Reid:	SEE MY NOSE.
T:	Steve, what could we do to figure out this word? *[Shows page with KNEE on it]*
Steve:	Chunk it.
T:	Can you try that?
Steve:	It's too small.
T:	What else can you try?
Steve:	Sound it out.
T:	What did you get?
Steve:	K—NEE
T:	Does that sound like a word we know?
Steve:	*[Shakes head no]*
T:	Chanel, can you help us figure out this word?
Chanel:	I know the word—KIN.
T:	Try that word and see if it makes sense.
Chanel:	Yes.
T:	Josh, what strategy would you use?
Josh:	I just sound it out in my head.
T:	What did you get?
Josh:	KIN
T:	Does it make sense?
Josh:	No.
T:	Lindsey, what else could we do?
Lindsey:	SEE MY KNEE.
T:	How did you know it was KNEE?
Lindsey:	It's a silent K.
T:	Let's look at one more word *[Shows page with MONSTER on it]* Kim, how could we figure it out?
Kim:	Sound it out.
T:	What did you get?
Kim:	MONSTER.
T:	How do you know that's right?
Kim:	I looked at the picture.

FIGURE 4.3 Abby's transcript

Student	Word Attempted	Miscue	Strategy Articulated	Strategy Used	Success	Cross-check	Insights
Carl	*fingers*	no guess	chunking	read past	none	—	needs strategy work
Sean	*fingers*	OK	—	chunking	yes	picture	OK
Kyle	*nose*	*noss*	none	sounding out	some	—	"vce" pattern
Reid	*nose*	OK	picture	picture	yes	reread	OK
Steve	*knee*	*k-nee*	chunking sounding out	chunking sounding out	some some	meaning	"kn" pattern
Chanel	*knee*	*kin*	none	sight	little	meaning (not successful)	"kn" pattern, strategy work, cross-check for meaning
Josh	*knee*	*kin*	sound	unclear	little	meaning (successful)	engagement level? "kn" pattern, strategy work
Lindsey	*knee*	OK	none	read sentence	yes	sound pattern—OK	articulating strategies
Kim	*monster*	OK	sounding out	unclear	yes	picture—OK	best strategies?

FIGURE 4.4 Abby's group grid

She could see that some students have a good handle on using word identification strategies, whereas others need more instruction.

Abby decides to reorganize the group and provide a follow-up lesson for only the students who need additional help with a particular strategy. Some students need further help with chunking, some need to practice graphophonemic patterns like "-vce" and "kn," and one needs to be reminded of the importance of cross-checking for meaning. In these smaller groups, she will actually demonstrate how to use several of the word identification strategies she recorded on the class chart. After she demonstrates a given word identification strategy, she will have students apply it with the books they are reading while she watches and assists as necessary.

Scenario 3: Juliet's Second Grade

About The Scenario

Juliet's second graders have been working on using story maps as a way to better remember story events. This scenario is an outgrowth of these whole-class lessons and takes place over two days.

Before the Guided Reading Experience

Juliet has taken a close look at the students' performance on using story maps to identify important elements in the story. She sees that they all have a pretty good handle on this, but she wants to give additional practice in applying the skill under her watchful eye. She has thought through the following five elements.

1. *Purpose:* Day 1—demonstration (literary elements);
   Day 2—shared response (multiple titles)
2. *Grouping technique:* Mixed achievement
3. *Text considerations:* Several titles all related to fall
4. *Text selection:* Student (from teacher preselected books)
5. *Time:* 30 minutes

During the Guided Reading Experience

Juliet begins by asking students to think about the parts of a story that most authors include. As students comment, she writes their ideas on the board. She then tells students that in today's story, the author has used a specific story map to write the story. She shows them the map (see Figure 4.5). Juliet notes that the main ideas they want to look for today are those that happen at the beginning, middle, and end of the story. She also reminds them that knowing this structure ahead of time can help them to better remember the story; it gives them a way to organize their thoughts.

She then provides a demonstration using the book *Fall Leaves Fall* (Hall, 2000). After she reads it, Juliet writes down one idea that was mentioned in each phase of the story saying, "Now let's see. There were a lot of ideas mentioned in this story. Let me think about what happened at the beginning, middle, and end." After she writes one idea for each part, she invites students to tell her some additional events that happened at each phase and then records their ideas.

Once she has demonstrated the process, she invites students to select a book from those she placed on the table. Each book is related to the fall season. She gives each student a copy of the story map (see Figure 4.5) and reminds them that one of their purposes for reading the story is to determine what happens at the beginning, middle, and end. Juliet then provides students time to read their books silently and to fill out their story maps. She assists as needed.

Names _____

The title of our book is _____

_____

The author of our book is _____

Beginning

```
┌─────────────────────────────────┐
│                                 │
│                                 │
│                                 │
│                                 │
└─────────────────────────────────┘
```

Middle

```
┌─────────────────────────────────┐
│                                 │
│                                 │
│                                 │
│                                 │
└─────────────────────────────────┘
```

End

```
┌─────────────────────────────────┐
│                                 │
│                                 │
│                                 │
│                                 │
└─────────────────────────────────┘
```

Adapted by permission of Juliet Sisnroy, Pueblo, CO

FIGURE 4.5 Juliet's story map

After the Guided Reading Experience

Juliet compliments students on how well they read and on their ability to recall information from various points in the story. She reminds them that the purpose for doing this activity was for them to be able to better remember what happened in the story and to develop a "mind map" similar to the author's. She emphasizes that, as they read other books, they can do the same kind of map in their heads to think about the story they are about to read. Taking time to do so before reading the story will help them remember it so that they can talk about it with others.

Juliet reflects on the lesson. She feels confident that students were able to discern events at the beginning, middle, and end of the story. She decides that she will offer a different guided reading experience tomorrow. Instead of demonstrating, the focus of the experience will be shared response. She will keep the groups the same and give each person a chance to talk about his or her book using the story map as a guide. She knows that doing so will not only help students know how to better articulate their ideas, but it will whet the appetites of others in the group. That is, as a result of hearing a bit about the books, other students in the group will want to read some of the additional titles. If time permits, she will then have students return their books to the middle of the table and let them choose another title to read. If time doesn't allow for this, she will keep the group intact for a third day to provide for this opportunity.

Scenario 4: Danette's Third Grade

About the Scenario

Danette is a third-grade teacher who recognizes the importance of providing small-group instruction that focuses on specific components of reading even for third-grade students. In this scenario, she works with a group of students who need to expand their repertoire of reading strategies.

Before the Guided Reading Experience

Classroom observations during self-selected reading have helped Danette to see that some students seem unable to use both meaning and visual clues to determine word pronunciation and meaning. Recognizing that she will get more student involvement if she works in small groups, she has thought through each of the five elements and is now ready to begin instruction.

1. *Purpose:* Demonstration (predicting and confirming)
2. *Grouping technique:* Mixed achievement
3. *Text considerations:* Day 1—One title, *Ramona Quimby, Age 8* (Cleary, 1992); Day 2—One title, newspaper article from *USA Today*
4. *Text selection:* Teacher
5. *Time:* 20 minutes

During the Guided Reading Experience

Danette begins by having students brainstorm answers to this question: "What do you do when you come to a word you cannot pronounce or do not understand when you are reading?" As students comment, she begins to create a semantic map on the board that shows their ideas. Once they have exhausted their ideas she asks, "How about using a couple of these strategies at one time? Let's give it a try." She displays the following sentence:

When we were camping last week, we saw lots of _____.

Then, she continues, "You'll notice that I have covered one word in the sentence. Let's read the sentence first and see if we can come up with some words that would make sense." She actually gives a suggestion and then invites students to do the same and writes their suggestions on the blank chart to the right of the sentence. Students suggest these words: bears, trees, plants, campers, trailers, tents, and campfires. She tells students that their choices show that they are using one important strategy when reading—making sense; all of their words would make sense in the text.

Danette continues, "But we also have to make sure that we pay attention to what the author has actually written. We can do this by looking at the actual letters of the word. Let's give it a try." She uncovers the first letter of the word (*wildlife*), asking, "If the first letter of the word starts with *w* can any of the words you suggested be right?" Students look at their chart and agree that while their word choices make sense, they cannot be used here because none begins with a *w*. Danette then asks, "So what could go here that would make sense that begins with a *w*?" Some students volunteer, "weeds, water, wildlife." She compliments students on using both meaning and the beginning letter to figure out the unknown word. Danette then uncovers the next letter (*i*) and asks students if any words need to be crossed off the list. They note that all but *wildlife* must be crossed off because the second letter in each is not an *i*. Danette crosses off the two words and then reveals the entire word, *wildlife*. She asks, "Is this the same word as the one we have on the chart?" She has students check and note the letters in the word. Then, she has them read the entire sentence to make sure that the word makes sense.

Danette provides other examples to make sure all students in the group know how to use both meaning and letters to figure out an unknown word. She concludes the lesson by giving them a passage from the book they are reading that has words partially deleted and asks that they read the passage and fill in the missing letters of the word so that it makes sense and looks right. She assists as needed.

After the Guided Reading Experience

Danette reminds students that the whole purpose of this lesson was to help them improve their reading by giving them different ways to figure out unknown words. She also reminds them that this is something they need to use when they read any text.

Danette reflects on the lesson. Her observations and the student's individual responses help her to see that this was probably enough for these particular students; they appeared to grasp the idea with relative ease. She recognizes that students need to be able to transfer this word identification strategy to the reading of informational articles. Therefore, she will follow the same basic plan tomorrow. This time, however, she will have the students read the article entitled "What's a Nurtia? A Really 'Nasty' Beast" from *USA Today*. It contains several challenging words—*culprit, fragile*, and *vulnerable*—which will afford students ample opportunities to practice predicting and confirming.

Scenario 5: Chuck's Fourth Grade

About the Scenario

It is the third week of the school year and Chuck has been having his fourth graders read different titles from the *Boxcar Children* series. He purposefully chose this series of books for students to read as a way of easing them into fourth grade. His past experiences have shown him that these books are fairly easy to read for most fourth graders.

Chuck also recognizes that having all children read a different book in the series, and then talking with one another about their book, is an excellent way to build a community of learners. He wants his students to see that they can learn from one another, and he wants every single one of them to see that they are valued class members.

Before the Guided Reading Experience

In looking at the curriculum established by the school district, Chuck sees that teaching fourth graders to discern likenesses and differences among books written by the same author is one goal. He decides to use the *Boxcar Children* series books to help him accomplish this task in addition to his goals. He has conducted numerous guided reading lessons with these books thus far, each based on his observations of students as they read and conferenced with him. However, the focus of today's guided reading lesson will be on likenesses and differences among the various titles. The majority of the students have nearly finished reading their books. Chuck has carefully thought through the following five elements for this guided reading lesson.

1. *Purpose:* Day 1—demonstration (literary elements);
   Day 2—shared response (multiple titles)
2. *Grouping technique:* Day 1—mixed achievement (large group); Day 2—mixed achievement (small group)
3. *Text considerations:* Multiple titles of the same series
4. *Text selection:* Students
5. *Time:* 45–60 minutes

During the Guided Reading Experience

Chuck begins with the entire class. He reminds them that each has been reading a different title in the *Boxcar* series. He tells them that today what they will do is discover how the books are alike and different. At this point he stops and asks, "So why do you think it would be important to focus on likenesses and differences among books in a series, all written by the same author?" As students start to give him their responses, he writes them on the board. Their responses include: to better understand the books, to create interest in all of the books, to get hooked on an author. Chuck states: "Yes! You have some excellent ideas about why we would want to know about how the books are alike and different. I'll let you in on another secret: knowing about an author's style can help you to read faster yet still understand what you've read. This can happen because once you're onto an author's style, you read with that author's style in mind. In fact, sometimes, you'll feel like you're reading the same book and all the author has done is change a few of the characters' names and a few of the events. The rest seems to stay the same. So you can read a bit more quickly. You can then have more time to read other books. All of this reading makes you even better readers because we know that lots of reading practice makes for better readers."

He then continues, "So let's think about the stories in this series: How do you suppose they are all alike?" As students state their ideas, Chuck creates a semantic map placing the words "Boxcar Children" in the center and their ideas on rays emanating from the center. He makes sure that the map includes the following elements: setting, Grandpa, new character, and plot.

The lesson continues as Chuck says: "Now that we've had a little time to think about how these books are alike, we're going to take a close look at these four characteristics: setting, Grandpa, new character, and plot. You will need to look back through your books to locate this specific information. Watch me. I'll show you how I did it with the *Boxcar Children* book I've been reading."

Chuck then takes them through the process and writes the information on four different colors of paper (one for each element), then affixes each under the appropriate heading on the chart (see Figure 4.6). He then provides students with materials and invites them to get started. As students read to locate specific information, Chuck circulates to provide help as needed.

After the Guided Reading Experience

Chuck compliments students on how well they were able to find specific information related to their text. He also tells students that the following day he will have different groups meet to discuss books so that everyone will have an opportunity to share with at least four other individuals. As they share, their information will be compiled onto a class chart.

Chuck reflects on the lesson. He was greatly impressed by the students' ability to locate specific information about their books. This tells him that they already have a pretty good handle on how to read looking for specific information. However, there are some students who appeared to struggle with this; he seemed to need to provide them with a lot of help. He makes note of these students and plans to design a guided reading lesson for them in the near future. What he wants to do now, however, is provide some time for students to talk with one another. He has noticed that although it is early in the school year, students are already starting to become creatures of habit; they are only interacting with a few students rather than all of their classmates. Recognizing this, Chuck will have students who normally do not interact with one another in the same group. In this way, they will have an opportunity to meet others in the class and to develop additional friendships.

Title	Setting	Plot	Grandpa	New Character
Boxcar Children (#1)	Ch. 1—Baker's Shop Ch. 2-8—Woods Ch. 9—Cherry Orchard Ch. 10—Park Ch. 11-12 Dr. Moore's House Ch. 13—Grandpa's House	The children are trying to live on their own, as their parents have died. They are independent and resourceful yet afraid of their grandpa.	He enters at the end of the story. He's looking for his lost grandchildren.	Dr. Moore. He helps the children by employing Henry.

FIGURE 4.6 Characteristics chart

Scenario 6: Mac's Fifth Grade

About the Scenario

Mac has been teaching fifth grade for several years. Every year he has noticed that his students' reading varies from those who are still reading fairly easy text all the way to those students who appear to be able to read just about any text that is put in front of them. He uses guided reading as a way to help address his diverse group of students. A master at classroom management, Mac has established several procedures to maximize learning throughout the day (see Chapter 5).

In this scenario, Mac has decided to use a common core selection from a basal reader anthology as a catalyst for helping students to read additional information in social studies and science. The text is an informational selection entitled "Yellowstone: Flames and Rebirth." It focuses on forest fires, one of at least four natural disasters to be explored during the unit on natural disasters. Mac wants to make sure *all* students are familiar with this text so that everyone will have a common experience with which to make connections throughout the unit.

Before the Guided Reading Experience

Recognizing that some students in the class will have difficulty with this text and others will not, Mac decides to invest time and energy to "frontload" the reading experience. *Frontloading* means that he will help all students by activating their prior knowledge, developing additional background information, addressing strategy needs, generating interest, and setting a purpose for reading. He knows that frontloading will help all students be better prepared for the reading to follow. Mac has also thought through the following five elements.

1. *Purpose:* Day 1—a combination of demonstration (strategy focus) and intervention (multiple differentiation); Day 2—shared response (single text with multiple parts)
2. *Grouping technique:* Day 1—mixed achievement (large group), similar achievement (partner reading and small group reading); Day 2—mixed achievement (large group)
3. *Text considerations:* Single text (basal reader selection, informational text divided into several parts)
4. *Text selection:* Teacher
5. *Time:* 60 minutes

During the Guided Reading Experience

Day 1

Mac begins by working with the whole class. He places a sheet with a chunk of the text on the overhead for all to see and begins working with it. Through think-aloud activities, he begins to model the strategies that good readers use to monitor one's understanding, find the main idea of a paragraph, and summarize the meaning in one's own words (i.e., paraphrase)—see Figure 4.7. He then invites students to assist him with this process.

Still in the large group, Mac guides the students through the reading of another text chunk. Through effective questioning, he supports students as they think aloud, revealing to their peers how meaning is monitored and summarized. He then shifts more of the responsibility for learning onto the students' shoulders by having them read the third chunk of text independently and state how they determined and summarized the important ideas. Walking around the room, Mac checks for understanding and provides support as students complete this reading. After providing this guidance to the whole group, he then shifts the instruction from the whole group to small groups because he knows that doing so will allow him to provide more guidance for those who need it.

Mac uses subheadings to divide the rest of the text into five sections, each of which can be read independently of one another. Rather than expecting all students to read the entire text, he assigns students to teams according to reading levels (i.e., general achievement). He gives each team their section with the expectation that they will read it and synthesize the information for the other students. Figure 4.8 shows these assignments.

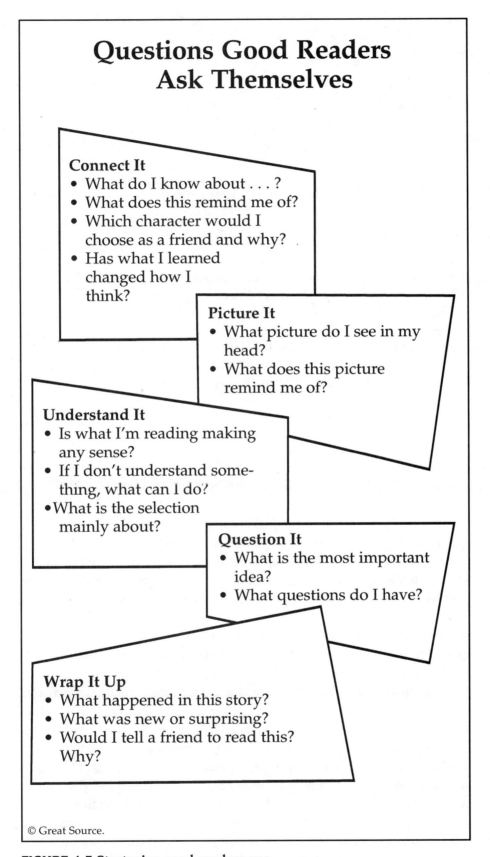

Questions Good Readers Ask Themselves

Connect It
- What do I know about . . . ?
- What does this remind me of?
- Which character would I choose as a friend and why?
- Has what I learned changed how I think?

Picture It
- What picture do I see in my head?
- What does this picture remind me of?

Understand It
- Is what I'm reading making any sense?
- If I don't understand something, what can I do?
- What is the selection mainly about?

Question It
- What is the most important idea?
- What questions do I have?

Wrap It Up
- What happened in this story?
- What was new or surprising?
- Would I tell a friend to read this? Why?

FIGURE 4.7 Strategies good readers use

Group Tasks

1. Read your section in one of these ways:
   - Everyone read silently.
   - Partner read.
   - In turn, have each read as others listen.
   - Listen to it on tape.
2. Record important details.
3. Record questions.
4. Summarize.
5. Be ready to share. Remember that other groups have not read your part!
6. Scan the rest of the article.
7. Look at other resources.

Team 1: Joe, Sally, Marie, Juan, Ted **Section of Text:** "Should we put it out?" (pp. 146–47)	**Team 2: Ed, Josh, Rachel, Sheryl, Pat** **Section of Text:** "Yellowstone Aflame" (pp 148–49)
Team 3: Barb, Alissa, Mike, John, Anna **Section of Text:** "Fighting Fires" (pp. 150–51)	**Team 4: Lisa, Rob, Jeff, Julie, Troy** **Section of Text:** "Aftermath" (pp. 153–56)
Teams 5: Autumn, Rick, Camila, Jose, Ed **Section of Text:** "The Future" (pp. 156–57)	

FIGURE 4.8 Planning sheet for the team reading of "Yellowstone: Flames and Rebirth"

Having the students read the text in this way enables him to assign given chunks of text to different teams based on difficulty and length. It also allows those students who can read and respond independently to do just that while at the same time enabling him to provide additional support for those who need it. That is, once teams, texts, and tasks have been assigned, he can provide support for those students who need it the most in a small-group setting. In the small group, Mac provides an intensive guided reading experience and assists students to read and respond to what might have been a difficult text had they not had his support.

Once in the small group, he tailors the guided reading experience more appropriately to the needs of the students. Mac selects a shorter, high-interest passage for the students who need his support the most. He begins by reviewing the graphic organizer to use in responding to the text. He models once again for the small group by reading the first paragraph of this section aloud to them and thinking aloud as he records the main idea and supporting details. Mac continues to provide support as this small group reads and responds to the remaining text. He simultaneously keeps his expectations reasonable and adjusts his support to help group members make sense of this section well enough to share it with others afterwards. After assisting this group of students, Mac checks to see that all others have finished their tasks. He reminds the groups to prepare their materials so that they can share what they have learned tomorrow.

Day 2

The class is brought back together. Each team shares what they learned from reading and responding to their section of the text. This shifts the instruction to a whole-class, mixed-achievement group of learners in which everyone is able to make an important contribution. After the discussion, the students are asked to respond to the statements in the previously completed anticipation guide to see if what they have read and discussed changed their feelings about these issues and ideas (see Figure 4.9).

Mac then asks all students to take a sheet of scrap paper and fold it in half. On one side his students write the word *THINK*, which he tells them stands for "Things I Now Know," and on the other side they write the word *WINK*, which stands for "What I Need to Know." He invites his students to reflect and write about what they have learned and what they still would like to learn about forest fires. He invites them to share their *THINK-WINK*s with partners. He then asks for volunteers to share their responses in the large-group setting.

ANTICIPATION GUIDE
for
FLAMES AND REBIRTH

1. All fires are bad for forests.

2. People cause the worst forest fires.

3. Fires hurt most living things in the forest.

4. The U.S. government's forest fire policy in national parks needs to be reexamined.

5. News people treat stories about natural disasters fairly.

State whether you
Agree (A)
Disagree (D)
or are
Unsure (U)
and
Why you answered that way

FIGURE 4.9 Anticipation guide for *Flames and Rebirth*

As they share, he records the students ideas and questions on a *KWHL* chart. In the *K* column he writes down facts they now Know. In the *W* column, he writes down What they would like to know. He guides them in reexamining the questions that have surfaced and records ideas in the *H* column—How they might find out the answer to those remaining questions. As the "how"s get identified, Mac begins to assign follow-up inquiry questions to teams, pairs, and individuals with the understanding that they will fill in the final column—What they learned—after they have had a chance to do some independent exploration of additional resources on forest fires.

After the Guided Reading Experience

Mac is pleased with how well these lessons went. Observations have revealed much! Students were able to work in their teams while he worked with the small group. He has worked with helping students know how to be independent learners and takes delight in seeing that all of this effort is paying off. Their independence enabled him to work with a small group of students who needed some additional help. He feels good about his instruction and recognizes that his plan enabled all students to experience success and to advance in reading.

When thinking about what transpired in the large group, he takes a look at the chart and thinks about the students who volunteered to respond to the whole group. As he reflects on the small-group portion of the lesson, he looks back on the notes he took to determine the kind of support he needed to provide to individual students within the group. This reflection will help him plan for the next day's instruction. He will take a close look at the informational texts he wants students to read as an extension of this lesson and determine how to lead students through it so that, like with the common core experience shown here, all can get something from a more independent reading experience.

Scenario 7: Patti's Fifth Grade

About the Scenario

Patti plans to launch a unit focused on animals. To best accomplish her objectives, she decides that she will engage students in a variety of large-group, small-group, and individual inquiry projects as they explore science and social studies content related to animals. She will also have students explore animal narratives in her language arts program. Doing so will help students see the differences among text structures and how each type of text can help them understand animals and the emotional impact they can have on humans.

Before the Guided Reading Experience

Patti decides that she will begin the theme by introducing all students to a quality example of a realistic fictional animal narrative. Recognizing that some students may find this text difficult to read, she addresses each of the following considerations. She wants to make sure that she provides them with ample guidance so that they, too, can get a lot out of the experience.

1. *Purpose:* A combination of demonstration (comprehension strategies and literary elements) and shared response
2. *Grouping technique:* Days 1–4—mixed achievement (large-group, small-group, individual reading); Day 5—similar achievement (small groups)
3. *Text consideration:* One common core text to launch the use of multiple texts in a genre study of animal stories
4. *Text selection:* Teacher and students
5. *Time:* 45 minutes for each of the five days

During the Guided Reading Experience

Day 1

Patti chooses Newbery Award–winning novel *Shiloh* (Naylor, 2000). She will use this as a common core text before inviting students to select and create their own animal narratives. To get all students to begin to think about animal narratives, she starts by reading a picture book called *Martha Speaks* (Meddaugh,1992). She comments, "Today I am going to read you a story about an animal. Your job is to listen carefully to this story to discover what the animal actually does." After reading the story, she invites students to talk about animal behaviors.

As they share their ideas, Patti lists the ideas on a chart that she labels "Usual animal behaviors / Unusual animal behaviors." Once students have shared their ideas, Patti tells the class about her dog, Sam. Using a sheet on the overhead, she lists his unusual behaviors. She then notes, "What I want to do now is use these ideas to create a story about my dog, Sam." Then, she proceeds to write her story, thinking aloud as she does so.

Now that students have watched Patti's demonstration, she asks them to think about something unusual that one of their pets or an animal they know does. She gives each student a different colored index card and tells them to write ideas on this card. Students are then grouped by like color and provided time to share what they have written.

Day 2

Patti reminds students of the activities they did yesterday and asks, "So what do you suppose those activities have to do with what we will do today?" As students volunteer their predictions, she writes them on a chart and comments, "We'll write your ideas here and revisit them later." She then introduces the novel *Shiloh* by using an anticipation guide. She gives each student three notes and states: "I am going to show you three statements. I want you to think about each statement and then write an 'A' if you Agree with it and a 'D' if you Disagree. Once you have responded to each of these statements, I will then ask you to come up to the board and put your ideas under the corresponding column for each statement. Here are the statements:

1. It is sometimes OK to take something that doesn't belong to you.
2. You should always tell the truth.
3. It is easy to tell the difference between right and wrong."

After students respond to each statement, Patti provides time for them to first talk to a partner about why they responded as they did. She then asks for volunteers to report to the whole group. Finally, she has each student, in turn, put their ideas under the corresponding column (Agree or Disagree) for each statement. To close the discussion, Patti tells them that these are the three major themes addressed in *Shiloh*, and that they might find themselves changing their minds as the story progresses. She notes, "This is what good readers often do when they read a story. They think about what might happen, form their ideas, and alter them as needed while they read the story."

Day 3

Patti reviews what students accomplished yesterday. She then tells students the purpose of today's lesson: "Yesterday we talked about three main themes that appear in *Shiloh*. Remember that I told you that good readers form some ideas before they start reading and adjust them as necessary as they get additional information from the story? Well, that's not all they do! They also start to focus on three ideas to better understand the story: details about the characters, setting, and the tension in the story."

Then, she shows students three large sheets of chart paper, which she has created for this lesson, with the labels *characters, setting,* and *tension.* Patti asks students to make a similar format in their response journals by turning the journal on its side and drawing three columns and labeling them *characters, setting,* and *tension.*

Patti is now ready to use a think-aloud to show students how they can use the author's words to get clues about the characters, setting, and tension. She reads the first two pages aloud to the students, stops, and returns to the charts, saying: "This is amazing! Just by reading the first two pages, I already have some ideas about the characters, setting, and possible tension. Let me see. On page eleven, the author, Phyllis Naylor, has introduced us to the main character, Marty, and his family, which includes his sisters Dara Lynn and Becky, his ma, and his dad. It's hard to tell much about the setting, but by the way they are talking and by what they are eating, we know that the setting is probably different from where we live. I am already sensing a little tension between Marty and his sisters, but even more between Marty and his dad over the issue of hunting."

She then reads the next two pages and stops, but this time she asks students to do what they just saw her do, saying, "Now it's your turn. Add some information to the characters, setting, and tension columns in your response journals for these two pages." Then Patti asks for volunteers to provide their insights about any of the three and posts their ideas on the charts started earlier.

To shift more of the reading onto the students' shoulders, Patti has the students assist her with reading. She puts a sheet with the next chunk of the story on the overhead projector and provides time for students to read it silently. She then invites students to read it in unison, recognizing that this is one way of helping struggling readers; it gives them additional practice and they get to hear fluent reading. As with the previous two sections, students add to their individual charts and to the class charts.

For the next chunk of the story, pages 13–16, Patti partners up students at random and invites them to read and respond to the next section of the chapter with their buddies just as they have done with the previous two sections. Patti closes this part of the lesson by complimenting students on how well they are picking up on author clues and how well they are reading with one another.

Day 4

Patti uses the characters, setting, and tension charts to review what students have accomplished thus far. Today she is going to use readers' theater as the primary mode of helping students understand the text. There are four parts that need to be read: Marty, Ma, Dad, and Narrator. She writes these names on enough cards so that each student can select one from a bag. After having students draw a card, she divides the class into four teams, grouping them by like character. She displays sheets containing the last two pages of Chapter 1 and shows students that she has color-coded their parts. What they are to do is rehearse the parts by reading silently. After providing rehearsal time, she has each group read their part aloud, readers'-theater style. As with yesterday's lesson, today's concludes by having students talk about the three elements and a new character. She directs the students to add his name to their charts.

By the end of this lesson, Patti feels that her students have a good foundation for the continued reading of this novel. Everyone knows about the main characters, the setting, and the potential conflict in the story. They all seem eager to continue their efforts to discover more by reading on.

Day 5

Patti divides her class into two key groups. Previous classroom observations, as well as observations from the previous four days, have enabled her to see that there are some students who could easily continue their reading of and responses to *Shiloh* more independently. There are others who still need the kind of help she has provided during the first four days. For this group, she sets up the expectations for the day.

Patti reminds the students that they should continue to think about what they are learning from the author about the characters, setting, and tension in the story. Plus, they should record more details to share with the whole class later in their response journals. She also tells them to think about their reactions to those three key ideas (telling the truth, taking something that doesn't belong to you, and telling the difference between right and wrong) and whether they might change their minds based on what the students are reading in the next section of *Shiloh*. Then she allows the students to work independently.

Then she calls a small group of students who need more support to the guided reading table. With this group, she reviews what was taught and learned the day before. Patti begins by reading the second chapter and uses a think-aloud to demonstrate what good readers do as they read novels to help themselves understand and respond. She guides these students in continuing to read the text and supports them as they discover more about the characters, setting, and tension in the story. After twenty minutes, she finishes her work with the students in the small group and they return to the large group. Then, Patti invites all the students to assist her in adding details to the charts posted at the front of the room.

After the Guided Reading Experience

Patti continues this pattern of instruction until all students have read and understood this common core novel. She allows them one week to read *Shiloh*. At the end of each instructional period, she reflects on which students need continued support and which students can operate more independently. By providing students with a solid foundation and ongoing structured activities to encourage continued reading, understanding, and response, Patti is able to turn over as much responsibility to as many students as possible. Then she can use her time to provide effective support to those students who need it the most. Patti set up two additional activities for students to work on when they have completed the classroom expectations for the day and find themselves with free time on their hands. The first is writing animal narratives, which are based on personal anecdotes, in a writers' workshop format; the second is completing inquiry projects by researching assigned animals individually and with partners.

Scenario 8: Joe's Sixth Grade

About the Scenario

Joe loves poetry and wants to pass his passion for it along to his students. While they seem to have a good handle on reading both fiction and nonfiction texts, he has noticed that they seem less comfortable reading and responding to poetry, let alone sharing it with one another. In this scenario, Joe engages students who have a high interest in poetry in helping others see that poetry is nothing to be feared; it can be read for enjoyment.

Before the Guided Reading Experience

Joe decides to use *Joyful Noise: Poems for Two Voices* (Fleischman, 1989). He selects six poems from the book and makes enough copies so that each student can have one of the six. He also makes an overhead transparency of the first poem, "The Grasshopper." He will use this poem to demonstrate how poems are written and how they can be read. Joe also thinks through these five considerations.

1. *Purpose:* A combination of demonstration (text structure) and shared response
2. *Grouping technique:* Mixed achievement (small and large groups)
3. *Text considerations:* Seven poems from a single text
4. *Text selection:* Students and teacher
5. *Time*: 45 minutes

During the Guided Reading Experience

He begins by saying, "Today we are going to be reading some poetry from this book. These poems are like none you have ever seen before! I'll read the title and you see if you can figure out how they might be written." Joe holds up a copy of the book and reads the title aloud, *Joyful Noise: Poems for Two Voices,* and asks, "So what do you think?" A show of hands indicates that several students want to respond. To engage learners, he has them turn to one another to tell how they think the poems will be written. He then calls on one person to share with the rest of the class. This student notes that she and her partner think that all of the poems are written in two parts because the title says "two voices." Others in the class agree, as does Joe. Then he adds: "You are exactly right. But not only are they for two voices. The author has written them so that sometimes the parts are read separately, sometimes they are read together, and other times the parts are read together even though the lines that are being read are different. Both groups really have to pay close attention to one another to keep the poem going so that it will make sense. Let's give it a try."

He displays "The Grasshopper" on the overhead transparency and reads it aloud to the students, pointing to the parts as he reads. Next, Joe divides the class into two groups and has one group read part one, the second group read part two, and assists by pointing to the lines on the transparency. Once students have read the poem a couple of times, Joe progresses to the next step.

"Now that you've had some practice with this, I am going to let you select one of these six poems to read." He holds up the poems and reads the titles, then allows time for students to select their poems. Joe has made enough copies so that once all students have selected, there will be six groups of four. When they're finished, he tells students that they need to group themselves by like titles. He also tells them about the group tasks: "Now that you are in your groups, please look up here so that you can see what I expect you to accomplish." He then displays the chart in Figure 4.10 and reviews it with the students.

1. Decide which two people will read part one and part two.
3. Read your parts silently.
4. Practice reading your parts.
5. Practice reading your parts together.
6. Keep practicing until you can read the poem without hesitating. The idea is that when you are sharing it with the rest of the class, you will read it so well that the rest of us will be able to understand the poem and create some images in their minds using the words in the poem as our guide.

FIGURE 4.10 Group tasks for a poetry lesson

As students begin accomplishing these tasks, Joe guides the reading by circulating and taking note of how well students are able to function in the group and with the actual reading of the poems. He stops and assists as needed. He provides students fifteen minutes for this practice.

After the Guided Reading Experience

Joe has the different groups perform their poems for the rest of the class. As each performs, he tells the rest of the class to listen carefully and use the words to create the image of the insect that is being described. His observations tell him that students were able to accomplish what was expected and then some. They ask if they can do another poem tomorrow!

Joe reflects on the lesson. Overall he is pleased with how students performed; however, he also noticed that every group could have been more fluent. They could have used more time to practice to bring their poems to fluency. He will do this activity again and allow for this extra time. Joe also realizes another shortcoming about the lesson. While he asked the students to use the words to create visual images, he now recognizes that he expected them to do so without showing them how. Tomorrow he will not only allow more time for practice, but he will also focus more on helping students understand just *how* they can use the words of the poem to create visual images. Joe will model this by using a think-aloud.

Scenario 9: Kerry's Sixth Grade

About the Scenario

Kerry has been teaching sixth-grade language arts for two years. She recently attended a staff development session at which she learned about using a structured focus workshop to guide students' reading. She learned that a *structured focus workshop* is one in which lessons are designed to teach students about specific literary elements. She also learned that such a workshop can be used to teach students how to function in groups—to teach group-processing skills. She now understands that the lessons can and should be planned for both a whole group and smaller groups. In fact, Kerry now realizes that using a combination of both large-group and small-group instruction is advantageous when designing guided reading experiences that are to take place within the structured focus workshop. She has been using the structured focus workshop approach ever since and both she and her students have experienced much success.

In this scenario, Kerry's structured focus workshop focuses on teaching students a variety of response formats and group-processing skills. Past observations have helped her to see that her entire class needs additional help with both. Her main goal is student independence; she wants students to be able to use the various response formats independently and to work well in groups.

Before the Guided Reading Experience

Kerry decides to focus on the literary element of characters along with the comprehension strategies that can best help her students better interpret characters. She will invite all students to choose a narrative story at their instructional level to read during the workshop. She feels comfortable inviting students to choose their own books because she knows that the majority of narrative stories have a central character. Therefore, all students will be able to participate in the activities even though they have different titles that represent their interests and overall reading level. She has also carefully thought through the following five considerations.

1. *Purpose:* Days 1–5—demonstration (literary elements, response formats, comprehension strategies, group-processing skills); Days 1–5—shared response (multiple texts with focused responses)

2. *Grouping technique:* Days 1–5—mixed achievement (large and small groups); Days 1–5—similar achievement (small groups)
3. *Text considerations:* Multiple texts with strong central characters
4. *Text selection:* Students
5. *Time:* 45 minutes daily

During the Guided Reading Experience

Day 1

Kerry begins by introducing the idea of attributes and attribute mapping as a way to interpret characters. Using herself as a model character, she shows the whole class how to create an attribute map (see Figure 4.11). She then provides time for students to do the same using themselves as characters.

She continues by reading *An Angel for Solemn Singer* (Rylant, 1999) and tells students to think about the attributes the author gives to the main character. Once she has finished reading the book, she asks students to provide some attributes about Solemn Singer and constructs an attribute map that reflects their responses. Finally, she encourages students to think about the attributes of the characters they will be reading about in their books beginning today.

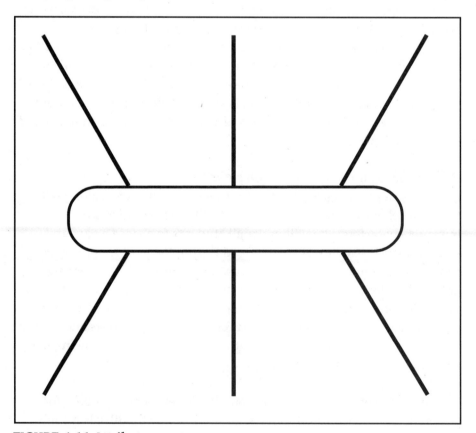

FIGURE 4.11 Attribute map

Kerry has them turn to a blank page in their literature response journals and tells the students that they need to prepare for today's reading by drawing a blank attribute map. She then tells them that as they read, they need to identify and add the name of the main character to the center of the map and begin to list attributes of the character on the lines extending out from the circle. She stresses that this map will begin today and will be ongoing and notes that many times the author will continue to develop the character throughout the story. She also says that some students may have found several attributes by the end of today's reading, whereas others may not; different authors provide information about their characters at different times.

Now, Kerry provides time for students to read silently. She checks for understanding and provides assistance during this time. After ten minutes, she gives them time to add to their attribute maps.

Day 2

Kerry is now ready for students to do some small-group work. She uses students overall reading levels to assign students to mixed-achievement groups of four. Once in the groups, she provides them with group tasks. Each group member is to tell about his or her book, focusing on the main character and the attributes of that character. As students go about completing these tasks, she pulls out a small group of students who seemed to need additional help yesterday when completing the attribute maps for their characters as they read silently. In turn, she asks each to name the main character in their books and asks them to state some attributes that tell about the character. As each does, she uses a whiteboard to demonstrate how to record this information on the attribute map. Students then record this information in their literature response logs.

After taking fifteen minutes for the small-group lesson, she uses the remaining thirty minutes for large-group instruction. She calls the class together and engages them in a discussion focused on character attributes. She asks for volunteers to share their characters and what they have learned about them. She also encourages students to assess how they did in their discussions: Did they stay focused? Were all members participating? Did all group members provide support for one another? She directs the students to turn to the next blank page in their logs and draw a line down the middle. On the left side she tells them to write *WE LIKE*; on the right side, she tells them to write *NEXT TIME*. She then has students write what they liked about their group participation and what they would like to do better next time.

Kerry recognizes that these quick self-evaluations can be revealing to both students and herself. She will look through their responses to help determine which group-processing skills to teach in the future. She plans to follow a similar format throughout the remainder of the week.

Day 3

On the third day, she introduces a response format that can be used to compare and contrast characters. Her guided reading lesson focuses on showing students how to compare and contrast literary characters with oneself and other literary characters. She shares an excerpt from *Dancing Carl* (Paulsen, 1995) and involves the students by having them complete a VENN diagram that compares Carl to Solemn Singer (see Figure 4.12). The purpose for today's reading and response activity is to emanate from this lesson.

After providing students with fifteen minutes to read silently, Kerry allots the next fifteen minutes for partner reading. She randomly pairs students and tells them to complete a VENN diagram to compare the main characters from their books. Students are encouraged to use their books and the previous day's attribute maps to complete this activity.

Kerry observes as pairs go about completing their VENN diagrams. Her observations reveal that there are two sets of partners that need additional help in understanding how the diagram works. She calls them together and takes them through the process once again. Then she has the four students complete the activity while she watches and gives help as needed.

Following the same format she established on the first day, Kathy concludes this guided reading session by calling the students together as a large group. She asks the students evaluate themselves.

Day 4

The fourth day helps Kerry to see that the students have read far enough in their books to notice that the authors are adding attributes to the characters,

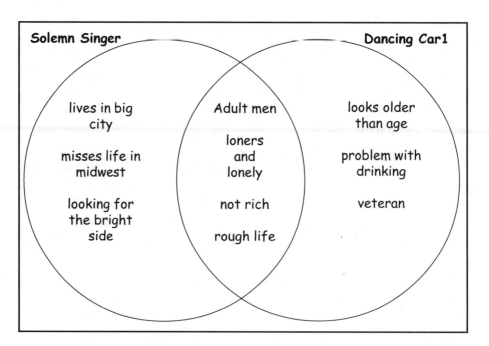

FIGURE 4.12 VENN diagram comparing story characters

thus causing them to develop and change. Recognizing this, she knows that this is an opportune time to introduce a response format—Character to a T (see Figure 4.13). She takes a blank overhead transparency and draws a big "T" on it. She labels one side "My thoughts" and the other "What the author said." Using *An Angel for Solemn Singer*, which she read on the first day, she actively involves the students as they identify what Solemn was like at the beginning, middle, and end of the story. As students share their ideas, Kerry writes them on the overhead sheet under the "My thoughts" column. She then asks students to listen for quotes from the book to support their ideas as she rereads. As these are identified, she writes them on the "What the author said" side of the chart. Students are then given time to read their own books and complete the "T" for their story's characters in their literature response logs. As during the previous three days, Kerry assists those who need more support. At the end of the day, all students are involved in the follow-up discussion and the group reflection.

My thoughts	What the author said
Beginning:	
Middle:	
Near the end:	

FIGURE 4.13 Character to a T

Day 5

On the fifth day, Kerry decides to pull out some good choices that an author made when selecting language to describe the character as the focal point of the story. She uses an excerpt from *Missing May* (Rylant, 1993) as an example. As with other lessons, she actively involves the students in listening and identifying good examples of character descriptions. She invites students to mark good character descriptions in their books with small stick-on notes as they read. She then provides students with fifteen minutes to read.

After they read, Kerry asks everyone to record the four best examples of character description in their journals. Like earlier in the week, she then randomly assigns students into teams and reviews the group tasks shown in Figure 4.14. After they share, Kerry creates a bulletin board and tells students that they can use this space to record additional examples of character description that they encounter when reading.

GROUP TASKS

1. Share examples of good descriptive language with your group.
2. Discuss which were the best and why.
3. Decide on four good examples from those shared.
4. Record the good examples on the overhead.
5. Star the one that is the best.
6. Be ready to share with others why you picked these examples.
7. When your group task is finished, keep reading in your book.

FIGURE 4.14 Group Tasks

After the Guided Reading Experience

Kerry reflects on the week's activities. She considers students' successes with use of the various response activities and decides which ones need more practice and which students can work independently. To decide how to group students in the near future, she considers which groups of students and partners worked well together. She also thinks about which group-processing skills need further attention. Kerry thinks about the students with whom she worked and considers whether they need more or less support. She checks over the notes she kept when monitoring the large-group discussions to get a sense about which student voices need to be encouraged. She looks at students' written responses to see what, if any, aspects of characterization need additional attention. All of this information will inform her thinking and actions as she plans subsequent structured focus workshops to be used for guided reading.

How Do I Remember What to Include When Planning for Guided Reading?

As the scenarios show, there is much to think through before the children arrive. One of the best ways to ensure their success is to plan for it. The lesson plan shown in Figure 4.15 is meant to be used as a guide to help you do just that. It shows the considerations that need to be thought through and provides space for you to write out what you want to accomplish at each phase of a lesson. Use the form as is or modify it to fit your unique needs.

Considerations	Teaching Strategies
Purpose: ___ demonstration ___ intervention ___ shared response ___ combination *Focus:* Strategy: Literary element: Procedure/process:	**BEFORE**
Grouping: Type: ___ similar achievement ___ mixed achievement Size: small groups of _____ Assign by: need interest random large group *Texts:* ___ commercial ___ children's literature ___ other	**DURING**
Number: ___ single title ___ multiple titles Title(s): *Text selection:* ___ student ___ teacher *Time:* ___ minutes for each group ___ minutes for whole class	**AFTER**

FIGURE 4.15 Guided reading lesson plan form

CHAPTER FIVE

Organization and Management

One of the greatest luxuries of small-group guided reading is the opportunity it affords to engage every child in meaningful reading experiences. It also enables you to observe all children and take note of how they read. These observations are invaluable because they reveal information that can be used to plan succeeding lessons. What's more, the small-group setting gives you the opportunity to help individual children as needed. Indeed, small-group guided reading is advantageous to both students and teachers.

All of this, of course, assumes that the rest of the children in the class are independently engaged with meaningful activities, know how to solve many of their own problems, and do not have to interrupt you and the group with whom you are working. Our teaching experiences and interactions with numerous teachers have helped us to see that, regardless of grade level, this independence does not happen by chance or magic but instead through explicit teaching. Regardless of grade level, children have to be taught how to work independently and what to do when they run into difficulties.

Clearly, the power of the instruction that takes place when students are learning independently must rival the power of the instruction that takes place with the teacher if all children are to maximize their full potential as readers. In fact, results of research studies designed to look at the factors that contribute to maximum reading growth among students have revealed that the best primary teachers achieve a 90/90 level of engagement in their classrooms—90 percent of the students focus on literacy tasks 90 percent of the time (Pressley, 1998).

In this chapter, we offer some suggestions to use to maximize the literacy learning that can and needs to occur during the time away from the teacher. These suggestions are aimed at addressing the teachers' question we hear most often: "What do I do with the other children when I'm working with a small group?"

How Do Learning Centers Help Me Organize and Manage Guided Reading Instruction?

Probably the most popular classroom structure that is used to engage learners when they are not working with the teacher in small-group guided reading lessons is learning centers—small areas within the classroom where students work alone or together to explore literacy activities. Students work in these centers independently. There are many ways to implement such centers.

Sometimes an entire reading/language arts block revolves around their use. One center is called "guided reading" and this is where the teacher is stationed. Children rotate through this and other independent centers according to a specified schedule during a certain block of time. This ensures that every child is provided with guided reading instruction each day and that every child also experiences the other centers as well.

In other classrooms, the structure is less comprehensive and less formal; children may or may not be grouped. They may be assigned to centers by the teacher or self-select to use them. The teacher forms a guided reading group by selecting children according to the purpose of the planned instruction. Instead of a set rotation, the remaining students are asked to stay at a center until a task is completed. Then, they are expected to select additional centers until the teacher is finished working with the guided reading group.

What Needs to Be Considered for the Effective Use of Learning Centers?

Regardless of the way learning centers are used, you need to consider their audience and motivation, how to foster independence, decisions about activities, the school system's expectations, and their overall structure. To ensure success for students and teacher alike, these must be thought through ahead of time.

Audience and Motivation

As with any good teaching, decisions about learning centers need to be grounded in what you know about the children as readers, writers, and learners. Looking at what children are able to do on their own and how they perform on assessments and during guided reading can provide a wealth of information. Next, you'll want to consider motivation. According to Brophy (1987), there are two keys to motivate learning: perception of the possibility of success and perception that the outcome will be valued. The instructional activities must be within the reach of learners. In other words, the learner needs to be able to perceive the possibility of success. Most of us quickly withdraw from an activity when we perceive that success is not possible, especially when that perception is based on the real experience of repeated failure. So it is with children. One way to set them up for success is to make sure that they fully understand the activity as the result of discussing, modeling, and practicing it in large- and small-group instructional settings. By the time the activity is placed in a center for independent use, students can't help but be successful.

Fostering Independence

In considering the learners, one often overlooked question focuses on independence. Just how well can the children function independently? What do they need to learn to function better as independent learners? Most often, children need to be taught *how* to be independent and taking the time to teach them is well worth the effort. For example, children may need to learn how to work with others in a group, use a tape recorder, care for materials, and/or locate help. To address needs such as these, lessons that focus on the procedural aspects of independent work can be designed, taught, and learned. Figure 5.1 shows a four-part lesson that we suggest you use. Figure 5.2 contains a scenario that shows the lesson's elements in action.

- A focus—purpose for the lesson
- An explanation—children are provided with information that relates to the stated purpose
- Role-playing—students have an opportunity for guided practice
- Direct application—children have time to use the information as they complete their centers' activities for the day

FIGURE 5.1 Four-part minilesson

Activities

Children need activities that will advance their knowledge about literacy in one or more ways. When determining which activities to use, the answers to questions such as these will lead to specific learning center activities to address them:

- Do students need repeated practice with a given story?
- Do they need to read with a partner to better understand a story?
- Do they need to write a response to something they have read?
- Do students need to listen to a given story on tape to better understand how to read with fluency?

You'll want to distinguish between independent activities that *generate* excitement about reading and writing and those that *engage* students in

Focus: Learning how to discuss

Explanation: "There's a lot to know about learning how to talk about a text with others. Today we'll begin to understand how to do this. What do you suppose a good discussion would look like?" As students state their ideas, the teacher writes them on a Discussion Etiquette chart. Their ideas include the following:

- Look at the person who is talking.
- Ask a question if you don't undertand.
- Take turns so that everyone can say something.

"You have a good start. Now let's give this a try."

Role-Play: The teacher invites four volunteers to join him in a discussion about a story that was previously read. What is important about this role-play is helping students to see how the ideas they generate come to life so that they will be able to do the same when they discuss. The teacher notes, "I now have my discussion group and we are going to start discussing. What the rest of you need to do is watch and listen to us and see if we are using the ideas listed on our Discussion Etiquette chart." A brief discussion then ensues, along with a debriefing in which students talk about which behaviors they saw.

Direct Application: To finish out the lesson, the teacher says, "So now that you know some ways to discuss with others and you have actually seen me do it with some of you, you need to do the same when you are discussing today. We'll keep our chart posted for all to see."

FIGURE 5.2 Sample lesson

reading and writing. While any number of cut, color, and paste activities done in response to or in support of reading and writing experiences can help to create some excitement about reading and writing instruction, these activities do little to engage students with actual reading and writing. Engagement with print is essential for learning about print and is what intensifies the power of center-based instruction.

State and/or District Curricular Expectations

Now more than ever, it seems that teachers are expected to follow curriculum guides and provide evidence that students have been exposed to, if not mastered, the curriculum. Designing centers with the literacy curriculum in mind is an excellent way to ensure that children are exposed to it. Of course, to make curriculum guides and documents user-friendly, you may want to transform them into manageable lists to keep at hand for easy reference. Such lists might be housed in a lesson plan book or affixed to a file folder. In some cases, activities can be coded to the lists.

Overall Structure

When thinking through the elements that can make or break using independent learning centers, the overall structure (i.e., *infrastructure*) requires some consideration. A learning center's structure needs to do the following.

- *Facilitate independent use by students*—Any activity that has the potential to interrupt small-group instruction because of the complexity of sustaining its operation may be more of a deterrent than a learning tool.
- *Operate with minimal transition time and management concerns*—If implementing centers consumes more time, energy, and effort than the instruction and activities that take place at the centers, using them needs to be rethought.
- *Encourage equitable use between activities and among learners*—If all center-based activities have value, it stands to reason that they will be important for all students. Although some students may like some activities more than others, they need to be encouraged to participate in all activities. If the organization precludes some students from having access to the same centers as other students, arrangements need to be made to equalize access.
- *Include a simple built-in accountability system*—Engagement in the center-based activities is critical if students are going to learn what we would like them to learn as a result of completing them. We know that some students stay productively engaged in the learning activities in the teacher's absence; but sometimes, we may well wonder whether *all* students stay productively engaged. Building a simple accountability measure will serve as a motivator for students to stay productively engaged and also serve as a "window" to each student's level of engagement. One accountability example is the center card which is issued to each student (see Figure 5.3). On it, a teacher can identify the independent activity options for students. As activities are completed during independent time, students write the date, and maybe the time, on the card.
- *Allow for efficient use of teacher preparation time*—Elaborate centers, which consume large amounts of teachers' limited preparation time without similar payoffs in the duration of student engagement time, will lead to a quick abandonment. What busy teachers need are structured activities that can be changed or altered easily once they've been established as part of center-based instruction.
- *Blend in with class routines*—Routines provide a predictable way for children to engage in learning and for teachers to plan instruction to

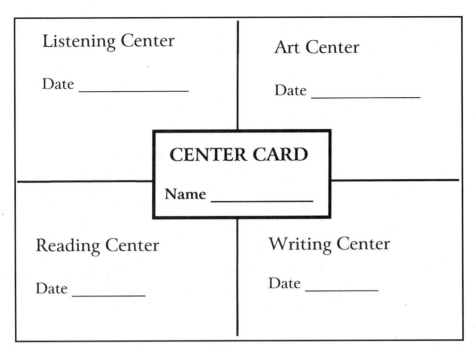

FIGURE 5.3 A sample center activity card

minimize concerns, confusion, and chaos. After they have been established and practiced, routines can be followed without teacher guidance. The gradual release of responsibility gives the teacher greater assurance that the activities students are expected to complete independently are within their reach. Posting schedules, such as the one shown in Figure 5.4, is one way to help children get a sense of routines. They also afford students with yet another opportunity to learn how to read different types of text—schedules.

What Are Some Good Examples of Literacy Centers?

What follows are descriptions of ten centers that meet the criteria just discussed. Next to each center name is the icon used to present the center in the remainder of this chapter. Each builds on classroom routines to encourage independent use by students and efficient use of teacher preparation time. While the structure of the center can stay the same, the activities within them can change with relative ease. Each is designed to be accessible for all students while providing for individual differences because of the level of sophistication each learner brings to the task. Each can be linked to what the teacher knows about students as readers, writers, and learners as well as to standards, curricula, and assessments as established by any given agency and/or staff. With simple structures, transition time can be kept to a minimum, equitable use can be encouraged, and accountability can be built in.

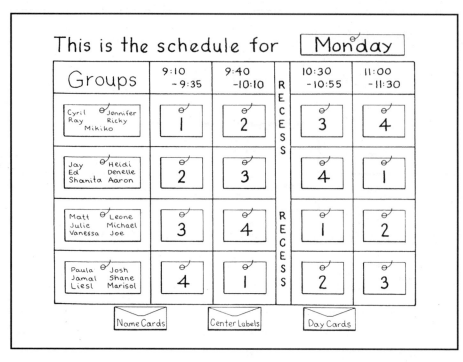

FIGURE 5.4 Sample schedule

Listening Post

The listening post is a perfect activity for an engaging independent center that provides learners additional practice with print. By placing a story on tape and multiple copies of the text at the center, the teacher can easily create a changeable center that provides learners an opportunity to warm up before, review after, or extend beyond a guided reading session. Sally, a second-grade teacher, takes it a step further. She intensifies the practice at the listening post by engaging students for a longer period of time that includes repeated practice of the text in a variety of ways (see Figure 5.5). She holds students accountable by expecting each one to orally perform a selection, which was practiced at the listening post, during sharing time at the end of the language arts block.

Listening Post

1. Listen to the story on tape and follow along.
2. Listen to the story on tape and read along.
3. Turn off the tape and read together.
4. Turn of the tape and read with a partner.
5. Turn off the tape and read on your own.
6. Listen to the story on tape and read along again.
7. Talk about your improvement.
8. Be ready to share the story with the class.

FIGURE 5.5 Listening post activities

Readers' Theater

Like the listening post, a readers' theater center is easily created by designating a practice space, providing multiple texts, and identifying guidelines for practicing. As with the listening post, it can be used as a warm-up, review, or extension from guided reading instruction. A readers' theater center can also be designed to encourage students of all levels to work together, because appropriate parts can be assigned to students of differing abilities. By providing a sequenced routine (see Figure 5.6), students are engaged for longer periods of time as they practice for a performance, which serves as an accountability check. This type of activity center provides a purposeful opportunity for building fluency, oral performance skills, and confidence.

The addition of simple props, masks, and/or puppets can make the production of plays from practiced texts another way to engage students. We have discovered lots of ways to create a readers' theater drama corner without investing a lot of time or energy in the creation of puppets or costumes. One teacher we know gathered old metal spatulas and character kitchen magnets and found that her students could easily make the puppets they needed by putting the appropriate character's magnet on a spatula.

Another teacher collected *grabbers*—character and animal heads on the end of a long stick with a handle that, when squeezed, causes the mouths to move up and down. Her children easily transformed these grabbers into the puppets they needed to perform a story. We even know of one teacher who ordered and used umbrellas that were shaped like the heads of animals—ducks, frogs, bears, bugs—the students used them as their "costumes" for dramatic performances. Again, because the students did not need to create complicated puppets, costumes, props, or scenery, they could spend more time staying engaged with reading the print and practicing for the plays.

Readers' Theater

1. Leader reads the story aloud.
2. Everyone reads the story together.
3. Partners read the story together.
4. Everyone is assigned a part.
5. Students practice their parts on their own.
6. Students practice their parts together.
7. Everyone gets ready to share the story with the class.

FIGURE 5.6 Readers' theater routine

Reading and Writing the Room

Reading and writing the room is a popular way to become familiar with a print-rich classroom environment. Students are encouraged to partner up and shown how to use special pointers and glasses as they read the room—

one student points to words in the environment as his or her partner reads them. Clipboards and scrap paper might be available for students to use in writing the room—copying down words about the environment.

Creating a scavenger hunt (see Figure 5.7) invites students to look for specific examples to explore concepts of print, letter names, word identification, and vocabulary elements. This is more closely grounded in curricular needs and is another way to engage students in a challenging activity. Hunts can be easily changed and/or designed with varying degrees of difficulty to accommodate for the needs of diverse learners. Usually, the students' efforts leave a "paper trail" that can be collected and quickly reviewed.

One of the easiest scavenger hunts for students is having them reexamine texts created or used in the class. The morning news, which is created collectively by a class, can be placed in a center and looked at for concepts of print (number of words, number of letters, number of sentences, longest words, shortest words, most frequent words, most frequent letters, and so on) or for word identification strategies (visual features of words, sound–symbol patterns, inflected endings, and so on). Clearly, hunts engage students in independent, meaningful print activities.

Scavenger Hunt

Find three words in our room that . . .

____ have more than six letters.

____ end in –ing where the final letter was doubled.

____ mean the same as "said."

____ have the same sound patterns as "boat."

____ are words from math.

____ start with "sh."

____ have the same spelling pattern as "nice."

____ are contractions.

____ rhyme with "she."

FIGURE 5.7 Sample scavenger hunt

Pocket Chart
Any instructional tool and space used in large-group instruction can easily become a center for more independent activity during guided reading instruction. In one classroom, the pocket chart is used to introduce common poems to be used as the basis of whole-to-part reading instruction. The print is started at the line, phrase, word, and word part levels. Figure 5.8 lists the procedures to show how it works.

1. Read the whole poem.
2. Invite students to reread the poem with you.
3. Write each line of the poem on a sentence strip (*done ahead of time*).
4. Invite students to use the sentence strips to reconstruct the poem in the pocket chart.
5. Provide students with words from the poem and have them place a word or words on top of ones in the sentence strip.
6. Give students a blank grid and have them copy each word from the poem into a box on the grid.
7. Once copied, have students cut apart the grid to make individual word cards.
8. Tell students that they can use these words to make a poem when they visit the pocket chart center.

FIGURE 5.8 Whole-part-whole pocket chart procedure

Because students have seen these activities modeled in a whole-group setting and have had some practice, they are more apt to be successful with them at the center. Students can also be shown how to work with partners and how word card games can be played by providing a number of opportunities for students to conduct independent skill practice with one another. Activities students choose can vary in difficulty according to their needs. The introduction of a new poem provides new material and another opportunity to repeat the activities.

Poems and Story Packs

Poems and stories can be used in several ways. One teacher we know retires a poem or story from large-group practice situations by placing the words, phrases, and/or sentences created for word study in a large see-through envelope. These packs of story and poem parts are placed in a basket and made available to students during center time. Because they contain materials created from texts of varying difficulty, students can select ones that are appropriate for their level.[1]

Students are directed to find a quiet place, to shake out the parts, and to engage in a variety of activities, including reconstructing the familiar text. Working with partners or independently, students engage in a variety of classifying and sorting activities that call attention to the words and their features. Words can be sorted according to visual or sound features, meaningful parts, and/or overall meaning. Students are also expected to record the words in their categories to show accountability.

---

[1] *Note:* Color-coding each text's parts makes it easy to get the right pieces back into the right pack!

Working with Words

Almost any working-with-words activity that is done in a large group can be transferred to a center once students have become familiar enough with it to be able to complete the activity with peer help or independently. When showing students how to make words by adding and deleting letters, for example, you can use an overhead projector and magnetic letters. While you model this in front of the class, students can have a "making words" sheet on their desks (see Figure 5.9). As words are generated on the screen, students copy the words into boxes on their sheets and then later add illustrations to show the meanings of those words.

Once this activity has been guided in the large-group setting a number of times so that students become familiar with it, it can be placed in the center. You need to identify an anchor word and place it in the center along with letter manipulatives. First, students manipulate the letters to create new words; then they record the words they create on the making word sheet and, if appropriate, add illustrations to show meaning. This recording sheet serves as an accountability measure.

Big Books

Revisiting big books used in shared reading experiences provides a natural opportunity for students to explore print more independently. Big books placed in an easily accessible center can be made more inviting by allowing students to also have access to teaching tools—pointers, word frames, stick-on notes, and correcting tape—so that they can conduct activities modeled by the teacher in the large-group setting. As anyone who has worked with young children knows, they thoroughly enjoy taking on the role of teacher.

FIGURE 5.9 Sample of a making words record sheet

Like texts created during routines, such as morning news, big books used during shared reading experiences can also be set up for scavenger hunts. A big book used in class can be identified as the center's book for a scavenger hunt (see p. 90). Students then examine the text for concepts of print or word identification strategies as they did with the morning news text.

Responding Through Art

Some students can best show their understanding of a selection through art. In one classroom, Shel Silverstein's poem *Spaghetti* had been featured. The response center contained a variety of bags of pasta and large sheets of colored construction paper. Students designed their own rooms and covered them in spaghetti in ways that were at least as creative as any teacher-prepared art project might have been. After adding print to their pages by labeling pictures, creating talking bubbles, or writing descriptive sentences, the student responses are used to first create a print-rich bulletin board and later bound into a book for the class reading center. The key with art response projects like these is to minimize the teacher's preparation time, maximize the students' creative abilities, and consider how adding print can provide more practice with reading and writing.

Writing

There is no question that one of the best ways to engage children with text is to have them generate their own. Writing demands much critical thinking because the writers must organize ideas and use specific words to express thoughts to create text that is meaningful to themselves and others. Other times, writing is a form of response enabling writers to show what was of personal value in the text or to show what was remembered. Certainly, it is a way for writers to apply all known print conventions. The centers can be easily created by supplying students with access to a variety of writing tools, formats, and resources. Students can engage in writing activities that differ in their demands. The writing projects can serve as an accountability measure.

Reading

We cannot emphasize enough that the best activity for students to become involved in away from the teacher is the activity they engage in with the teacher—reading. Students should always be encouraged to read when they are waiting for instruction. Reading practice can be done individually, with a classmate, or with a more competent coach. It is easy to create inviting reading centers that provide easy access and adequate opportunities to independently explore texts, which is another way to warm up, review, or extend guided reading instruction.

Students should be encouraged to grab a text, a buddy, and a carpet square from the stack in the classroom; find a quiet corner; and read to each other. Having other people in the classroom can provide the students with the possibility of additional contact with a competent reader—an older student or adult classroom volunteer. These individuals may not be capable of conducting a separate guided reading group, but they can certainly listen to individuals read. For accountability purposes, students can keep a record of the books they have read.

Additional Centers

In addition to the ten specific centers described here, the ones listed in Figure 5.10 are suited to a variety of grade levels.

- Computer workstations
- Retelling center for storytelling, reports, and radio announcements
- Content area centers for related math, science, and social studies
- Commercial and teacher-made print and language games
- Print-enriched dramatic play centers with literacy props
- Whiteboard, blackboard, and chalkboard activities
- Block areas enriched with materials for planning and labeling
- Music center with materials to read and create books based on songs
- Newspaper and magazine center with related activities
- Overhead projects set on the ground

FIGURE 5.10 Ideas for additional centers

Can Any Other Organizational Structures Be Used During Guided Reading?

Guided reading and learning centers are not inseparable components—we can have one without the other. Independent activity can be structured for students without relying exclusively on learning centers, but we want to avoid returning to the stacks and packs of worksheets and workbook pages that were used in the past as a way of keeping students busy when not with the teacher. Two ways to envision independent activities for students—alternative independent project formats and a new vision for "work folders"—are described next.

Alternative Independent Project Formats

Instead of setting up a variety of learning center activities, it may be more appropriate to consider the development of an independent project format that can guide students in self-directed, meaningful inquiry projects away from the teacher. Early childhood educators Harris-Helm and Katz (2001) have made this the foundation of their curricular approach—"The Project Approach." Even when such activity is not used as an entire curricula's approach, it can be planned as an alternative to center-based activities.

For example, one district we know of provided teachers with staff development time to pull together a consistent set of guidelines, rules, forms, and assessment tools that could be used to introduce an independent project format to all students within and across grade levels (see Figures 5.11a, 5.11b, and 5.11c). As a result, throughout the school, self-directed, independent inquiry projects became a familiar option for students when they were not working directly with their teachers.

GUIDELINES FOR INDEPENDENT INQUIRY PROJECTS

You are expected to follow these rules as you work on independent inquiry projects:

1. When working on your project, stay on task. Conference with the teacher before starting a new project or setting aside a planned project.

2. Wait to talk to the teacher until the teacher is not working with a group or another classmate.

3. Consult with other students to help you with your project if you are waiting for the teacher, but try not to interrupt their work.

4. Use inside voices when talking to each other about your independent inquiry projects during class time.

5. Use the pass system when you need to leave the classroom to work on your projects.

6. If you work outside the classroom, follow the rules of that area and the adult in charge.

7. Since independent projects are a special opportunity for learning for individuals, avoid calling attention to yourself by boasting about your work and/or privileges.

When working on an independent inquiry project, I agree to follow the rules above. The consequence for not following the rules will be the suspension of independent study privileges.

Teacher's signature _____

Student's signature _____

a.

SPECIAL PROJECT PLANNING SHEET (PRIMARY GRADES K–2)

Student's name: _____

Date: _____

Special topic: _____

What I want to learn: _____

_____

_____

_____

_____

How I will share what I have learned: _____

_____

_____

_____

_____

_____

Deadline: _____

b.

INDEPENDENT INQUIRY PROJECT PLANNING SHEET (INTERMEDIATE GRADES 3–5)

Student's name: _____ Date: _____

The topic I have decides to learn more about is _____

My reason for learning more about this topic: _____

_____

_____

Material resources I expect to use in my inquiry: _____

_____

_____

Human resources I expect to use in my inquiry: _____

_____

_____

What I expect to learn from my inquiry: _____

_____

_____

How I expect to share what I have learned: _____

_____

_____

Deadline: _____

c.

Adapted from *Teaching Gifted Kids in the Regular Classroom* by Susan Winebrenner (Minneapolis: Free Spirit Publishing, 1992) as suggested by use in the Fort Atkinson (WI) School District *Teacher and Student Guide to Independent Study.*

FIGURE 5.11 Sample district project formats

Although a district or schoolwide effort is admirable because it provides the advantage of a network of teachers working together to create a cohesive alternative to using learning centers, individual teachers can do the same. This is exactly what Brenda did in her first-grade classroom. She developed a simple planning sheet, introduced it to her students, and allowed them the option of designing their own independent projects to work on when they were not with her (see Figure 5.12).

THIS IS INTERESTING TO ME!

I would like to know about . . .

_____

_____

To learn about this I will . . .

_____

_____

Here's how I will let you know I have learned something . . .

_____

_____

My plan of action is . . .

_____

_____

I will be ready to present it to the class by _____

Student _____

Teacher _____

FIGURE 5.12 Brenda's project format
(Adapted from Brenda Wallace, Ashwaubenon, WI.)

Kim designed something similar for her third-grade students (see Figure 5.13). She also created an assessment sheet that asked students first to self-evaluate the project and then to share completed projects with their peers and family before turning them in to her. This allowed projects to pass through multiple levels of review before being evaluated by the teacher.

Harvey (1998) provides teachers with yet another vision of how such independent inquiry projects can provide older students with an engaging alternative to center-based activity during independent worktime.

A New Vision for "Work Folders"

Students can be provided with a "work folder" to guide independent work but rather than containing several worksheets or workbook pages to accomplish, this folder can contain a variety of reading and writing tasks. In one classroom, for example, students were exposed to a variety of poems as shared reading experiences. A copy of each poem was then placed in the students' folders for additional oral reading practice to further develop reading skills, such as fluency and oral interpretation.

Students also created a set of word cards based on the words in each poem. After working at the pocket chart to create the word cards, students

```
┌─────────────────────────────────────────────────┐
│              RESEARCH PROPOSAL                    │
│                                                   │
│  Name: _____ │
│  Title: _____ │
│  Author: _____ │
│  One subject that I read about in this book and   │
│  would like to find out more about is: _____ │
│  _____ │
│  My plan for doing so includes:_____  │
│  _____ │
│  What I will do to show what I have learned: ____ │
│  _____ │
└─────────────────────────────────────────────────┘
```

```
┌─────────────────────────────────────────────────┐
│              Evaluation of My Book                │
│                                                   │
│  My name _____ My book _____ │
│  Type of response _____ │
│  Was it: excellent _____ good _____ fair _____ poor _____ │
│  Neat _____ │
│  Complete _____ │
│  Understandable _____ │
│  Appropriate _____ │
│ - - - - - - - - - - - - - - - - - - - - - - - -   │
│           Evaluation of a Friend's Book           │
│                                                   │
│  My name _____ My friend's name _____ │
│  My friend's book _____ │
│  My friend's type of response_____ │
│  Was it: excellent _____ good _____ fair _____ poor _____ │
│  Neat _____ │
│  Complete _____ │
│  Understandable _____ │
│  Appropriate _____ │
│ - - - - - - - - - - - - - - - - - - - - - - - -   │
│           Parent's Evaluation of a Book           │
│                                                   │
│  Student's name _____ │
│  Name of book _____ │
│  Type of response _____ │
│  Was it: excellent _____ good _____ fair _____ poor _____ │
│  Neat _____ │
│  Complete _____ │
│  Understandable _____ │
│  Appropriate _____ │
└─────────────────────────────────────────────────┘
```

FIGURE 5.13 Kim's project format
(Adapted from Kim Brown, Oshkosh, WI.)

placed the cards in a zip-up bag inside their work folders to use to practice word card games and activities. The students were also given a list of each poem's words, which could be practiced and used in word games as well. The directions for additional projects linked to each poem, such as self-illustrated books based on the poems, were also placed in the work folders.

At any given time, the work folders always contained something that the students could work on while they were not working with the teacher. They could reread their poems, work with the word cards, practice with the word list, or complete a special project. In this classroom, a simple accountability system was developed by providing each student with a grid containing boxes for each poem, set of cards, word list, and special project. As students demonstrated competence in each activity, they were checked by the teacher and students were told to color in the box for the poem's activity that they worked on, signaling completion of that task (see Figure 5.14).

Miss Hocket Poem	Sea Serpent Poem	Spaghetti Poem	Bug on the Teacher Poem
Miss Hocket Cards	Sea Serpent Cards	Spaghetti Cards	Bug on the Teacher Cards
Miss Hocket Words	Sea Serpent Words	Spaghetti Words	Bug on the Teacher Words
Miss Hocket Project	Sea Serpent Project	Spaghetti Project	Bug on the Teacher Project

FIGURE 5.14 Student poem recordkeeping grid

Additional Organization Structure Ideas

As seen in the scenarios presented in Chapter 4, many teachers integrate guided reading experiences with other classroom organizational structures. Whole-group instruction of common core texts can follow a "grouping without tracking model" (Paratore, 1990). With this model, the actual reading of the text can be done by some students with the support of the teacher in guided reading groups, while others read the text without the direct support of the teacher. Activities can be structured so that while some students receive teacher supervision in a guided reading group, others can operate independent of the teacher.

Some schools have chosen to integrate guided reading into more process-oriented reading–writing program blocks such as with readers' or writers' workshop. Some children may be working with the teacher in small guided reading or writing conference groups, while others are working more independently with peers or partners doing their own reading and writing.

Some teachers have found that organizing and managing guided reading instruction is much easier if they can work with the other professionals in their classroom. They can assist students with special needs, language differences, or other reading difficulties. In inclusive classrooms with "pull-in" support models, a second pair of eyes, ears, and hands provides a more efficient way to manage all the demands of guided reading.

What Will Help Me Manage Accountability, Recordkeeping, and Assessment When Students Are Working Independently?

In Chapter 2, we briefly addressed the issue of assessment, discussing issues to consider in making decisions about the use of groups during guided reading. In addition to those ideas, the following are a few more techniques to consider to manage students and activities during guided reading time.

Punch Cards

Punch cards are a simple management system that can be developed and introduced to students to help manage and keep track of their activities while away from the teacher. To create a punch card, the teacher identifies four to eight independent activities—some may be at centers, others may not—that the students can work on when they are not being supervised. These activities are identified by icons in boxes on the punch card. You can also place numbers in the boxes (1, 2, 3) with each icon to indicate the number of times a student may complete that activity. The card is then duplicated and distributed to each student.

When students have choice time away from the teacher, the punch card serves as a concrete reminder of what activities can be done. As the students complete an activity, they can mark off the box in a number of ways to keep a record of having done it. The use of the punch card helps regulate the independent behavior of the students and facilitates the teacher's recordkeeping (see Figures 5.15a and 5.15b).

Folder System

A folder system is another way to keep track of individual students and their work. Expanding folders with multiple slots are available from any office supply store; they offer an easy-to-use place to collect and store student work until it can be reviewed. Each slot can be labeled over and over with students' names. As students complete work samples, they can file them in their own slot in a centrally located expanding folder. When the teacher is ready to examine the students' work, it is already collected and filed in one place.

Live Performances

Accountability for some independent work might be best handled through live performances. Building in a little bit of sharing time at the end of each language arts period is a good idea. This will provide students with the opportunity to share performances rehearsed at the listening post, readers' and/or puppet theaters, or for interpretive pieces worked out independently by individuals and partners.

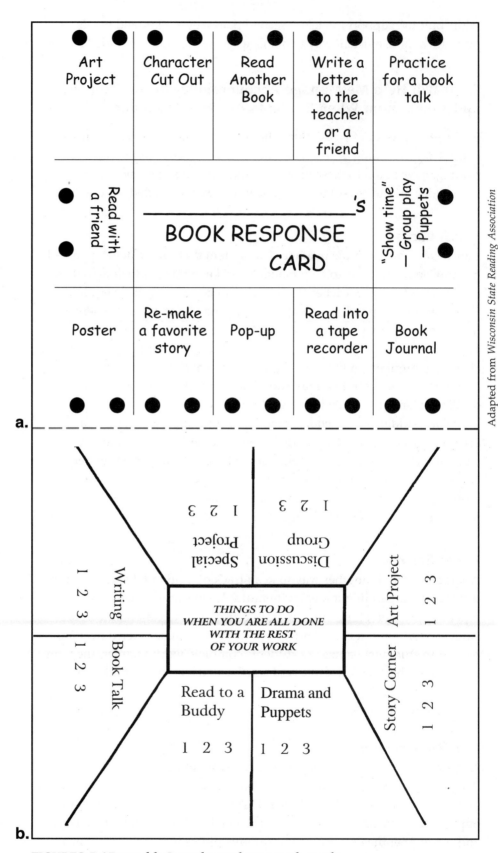

FIGURES 5.15a and b Sample student punch cards

Recorded Readings

When it is impossible to listen to all students, some may be asked to read into a tape recorder thereby recording the readings on audiotapes. These tapes can be analyzed at the teacher's convenience or by trained support personnel. The tapes can also be saved throughout the year to provide evidence of a student's progress.

Guided reading experiences can actually be built around listening to taped readings as students are invited to follow along in a text and uncover and analyze miscues they hear on the tapes. This may be particularly helpful for older readers as seen in *Retrospective Miscue Analysis*, a technique described by Goodman and Marek (1996).

Learning Logs and/or Response Journals

Integrating the use of learning logs and/or response journals as a tool for students to record independent work activities creates a space that is easy to collect and monitor. Students get into the regular habit of bringing their journals with them as they move through centers or complete individual activities. If students' journals are color-coded, separating them into five groups, you can be very systematic about collecting and reviewing journals without overwhelming yourself. A different color for each day identifies which ones to review on that day.

Again, making sure activities are structured so that they require some recorded evidence is critical. For example, instead of having students simply sort word cards at a working-with-words center, expect students to record the sorted words into categories in their journals. This work can also be collected in color-coded folders or prepared for more extensive presentations in color-coded portfolios.

Observation

To determine whether all students are actively engaged when not working under the teacher's direct supervision, frequent observation is a must. During the brief transition time, as one group moves out and another moves in, you can scan the "rest of the field." One helpful tool is to keep a class-list-type of observation form that has been created with the students' names on the left and blank space on the right. In a systematic scan of the class, starting at the top of the list and noting with a plus (+) or a minus (−) whether the student is engaged, you will begin to identify a profile for all the students. Even if you can't observe each student during each brief break, by systematically moving down the list you will eventually get a "snapshot" of each student's level of engagement.

Teacher–Student Interaction

Students whose profiles indicate difficulty with self-engagement and regulation may require more formal interaction during brief transitional periods or throughout longer blocks of independent worktime. Again a separate sheet with space to record interactions with these students will help the teacher more systematically monitor and regulate students' behaviors.

Recordkeeping Devices

To manage the collection of anecdotal information during conferences and other interactions and observations, we described two systems in our discussion of assessment in Chapter 2. Teachers have created flip chart folders by taping down overlapping index cards (one for each student) on the inside of a file folder. Each card contains the name of one student and the folder is a convenient place to record anecdotes while working with students. Another technique involves the use of blank mailing labels placed on a clipboard. Again each can contain a student's name and become a place to temporarily record information about a student. The labels can then be peeled off and stuck on the appropriate individual's folder.

Sharing with Others

Remember that you can relieve some of the concerns about management and accountability by sharing the responsibility with others. By introducing, developing, and implementing the use of well-defined rubrics to use for evaluating work, you can add a layer of peer evaluation and self-evaluation that will help to hold students accountable for the quality of their work. Just as having other professionals in the classroom is helpful sometimes, sharing concerns about students and asking for feedback about your evaluations of them may be very useful.

How Can I Reduce Student Interruptions When Teaching Groups or Individuals?

Many students take comfort in knowing that they can depend on their teacher when they encounter difficulties. As teachers, we like to help students. Put these two together and we are bound to get several interruptions.

Even though we want students to know that we are there to help them, we also need to show them how to solve their own problems whenever possible. Doing so will not only minimize interruptions but will also foster independent learners and learning. The following are some suggestions.

1. *Make it clear that you are not to be interrupted during a guided reading group.* There is nothing wrong with setting down some important parameters and then making sure that they are followed by everyone. You must get good at ignoring students who may approach you while you are working with a small group or individual. Investing some

time in role-playing so that students can see and hear what interruptions look like and sound like may provide them with better insights into why they need to be avoided.

2. *Encourage students to ask peers in their group their questions.* Certain students might even be identified as resource people during the guided reading instruction. A button, pin, or hat might clearly identify a student as the "question answerer of the day."

3. *If you have access to parents or other adult helpers during this time, identify them as the person to go to with questions.* You might also consider establishing a cross-age arrangement with a class of older students who could be used to field questions. It is important, however, to make sure that any additional resource people fully understand your processes and procedures so that they can address questions without interrupting you.

4. *If your students are asking a lot of questions about particular centers and activities, it may indicate that students are not ready to handle the activity either because of inadequate preparation or limited abilities.* You may need to stop using that center and practice it in a large group before turning it back to the students.

5. *Stay aware of typical interruptions and try to circumvent them before they happen.* With young children, for example, problems with materials and supplies can lead to many interruptions. Pencils break and disappear at a rate that can exhaust us. Having a supply of already-sharpened pencils available to replace those that somehow get lost is one way to anticipate and avoid a common interruption.

6. *Respond to legitimate questions during brief transitional times.* Students with questions might sign up on the board and when you are freed up, you can follow-up with those students whose names are on the board. Students might also have an indicator, like a folded card with a question mark on it, to set out on their desks. Then, when you quickly pass around the room during a brief transitional break, you can help those students.

"Yeah . . . But . . . What About These Questions?"

In this chapter, we have addressed questions commonly asked about organizing and managing instruction away from the teacher during guided reading. Our interactions with educators in a variety of staff development situations have helped us to identify a few more questions that typically surface. Usually those questions come from teachers who agree with what we have shared here ("yeah . . .") but always have at least one constraint, hurdle, or obstacle that prevents them from taking that first or next step (. . . but . . ."). Let's take a look at a few of those "yeah . . . but" questions.

■ *I see the value in using learning centers during guided reading, but my classroom space is too limited to accommodate centers. How do I manage space concerns in a small classroom?*

As stated earlier, keep in mind that one does not have to view guided reading experiences as inseparable from center-based instruction. There are alternative ways to engage students away from the teacher that do not rely on centers. But if you see center-based instruction as the best complement to guided reading experiences in your classroom and space is a real constraint, try one or more of the following suggestions.

1. Create centers that require a minimal amount of set-up space. Focus on what is needed for the learner. Worry less about display for the sake of appearance.

2. Create portable centers that can be moved to any open space. Placing center materials in tubs can help both to keep the centers organized and to make them transportable. There is nothing wrong with students taking the materials to their desks and working in that available space by themselves or with a partner.

3. Think about using spaces you might not first consider. Accessible lower cupboards when opened up provide surfaces that can be transformed into centers. The sides of steel file cabinets are perfect for using magnetic manipulatives. Velcro® strips and self-stick posterboards can turn wall, door, and room divider surfaces into centers.

4. Use existing instructional tools and spaces as centers when they are not being used for group instruction. The pocket chart, big-book stand, overhead projector, flannel board, and puppet theater can all become centers where students can replicate and innovate on the teacher's practices in the same spaces.

5. Students can work on the floor. Old tablecloths can quickly define and enhance a space for students on a cold tile floor. In-progress projects can easily be transported off the floor as needed by lifting the tablecloth. Puzzle mats, which avid puzzle builders use to roll up their in-progress efforts, might work similarly for ongoing student projects.

6. Grouping individual desks together can provide a tablelike surface that's more conducive to partner and team projects. Consider factors like that as you work around space constraints when arranging your classroom environment.

7. Allow more independent groups to be in the hall or with an adult helper. Students who have become good at reading and writing the room (see description earlier in this chapter) might be given a chance to read and write the hall. Scavenger hunts designed for the room could also be allowed to spill over into the hall. As we described before, a stack of discarded carpet squares can define quiet spaces for students to work individually or with their partners, even in a hall.

8. Remember, some of the best "centers" may actually be outside of your classroom. School policies that allow responsible students to visit and work independently in the library, media center, or computer lab create such opportunities. Preestablished pass systems and access to easily set timers can assist with transitions to and from the classroom to other school facilities.

■ *How can I keep track of which students need to go to which centers? Is there an easy way to set up a rotation schedule for centers?*

As mentioned, simple systems, such as the punch card, may be the easiest way to ensure that students rotate through all centers. Once a box has been colored in or punched, the student needs to select another center or activity. By using numbers that are punched out or crossed off, the student knows how many times they can visit the same center before having to try a new activity (see Figure 5.15).

In another classroom, the teacher uses a center wheel. Her independent activity options are identified on segments of an inner wheel; her small groups are identified by names placed on the outside of the wheel. By simply rotating the internal circle of activities, she automatically and systematically reassigns her students to new centers (see Figure 5.16).

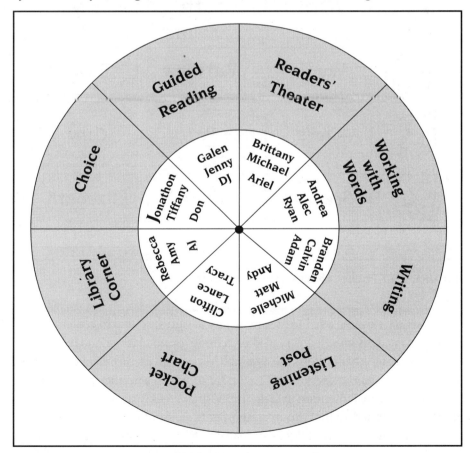

FIGURE 5.16 A center wheel

Another teacher uses a pocket chart that is devoted to center assignment. Icon cards are created for each independent activity option and placed on the left side of the pocket chart. Name cards for each of the students in class are placed to the right of each icon, thus assigning them to their center activity for the day. By simply moving the activity icon cards up in the pocket chart, students are systematically reassigned to new centers. When certain groups need their membership readjusted, the teacher only has to move the name cards to get the new assignments in place (see Figure 5.17).

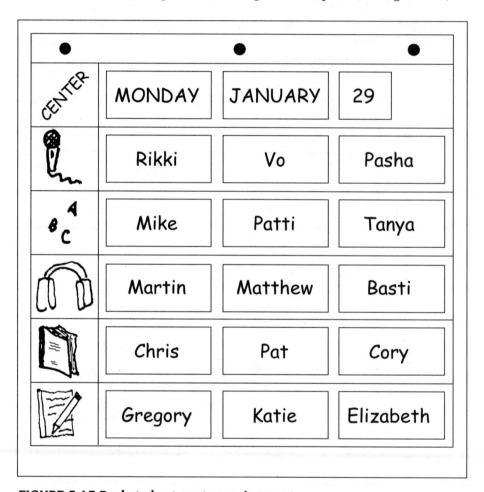

FIGURE 5.17 Pocket chart center assignment

Calendars can be used to automatically assign students to centers and independent activities. Icons placed on a large group class calendar reminds students about what options are available on any given day. Leaving the icons on the calendars serves as a reminder of which activities have been receiving the most attention in class. Individual weekly or monthly calendars might be designed so that group assignments are built into each one. These can be attached to desks, folders, or learning logs to remind students of their work activities and places for the day (see Figure 5.18).

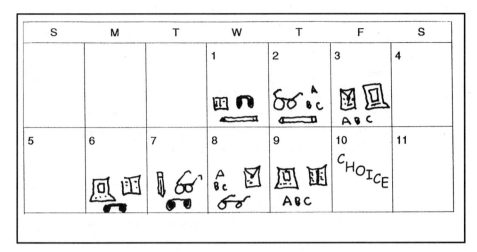

S	M	T	W	T	F	S
			1	2	3	4
5	6	7	8	9	10	11

FIGURE 5.18 Class calendar

Finally, remember that there is nothing wrong with letting students self-select their activities and center assignments. This is one way to discover which centers fall short of students' interests and expectations and may need to be rethought for future use.

■   *I see the value in guided reading experiences for most of my students, but what about special needs students who tend to challenge me the most in effectively implementing programs like this? What are some options for the special needs students in inclusive classrooms?*

In our work with teachers of special needs students whose reading and writing instruction is taking place in inclusive classrooms, they were unified in their opinion that their students should be held to the same expectations as the other students. The teachers weren't suggesting that these students might not need more support, more training, or more practice; however, they wanted regular classroom teachers to have high expectations for the students and to help them make progress toward goals established for other students. They were especially emphatic about making sure that the special needs students were working on reading and writing during reading and writing time. The following list contains some suggestions for accommodating students with identified exceptional needs.

1. For students with identified exceptional educational needs, it is important that individual education plans (IEP) clearly identify the goals and activities for the students during inclusive class instructional periods. All educators involved in supporting the students need to agree on what should be happening in a block like guided reading time.
2. Develop more detailed behavior plans and/or checklists that can be used to guide and monitor the students during these instructional periods. For example, if the students were to be integrated into small

discussion groups, they might be given four behavior cards (comment, opinion, question, and compliment) to take with them to the group activity. These cards can be concrete reminders for the students who struggle somewhat with social interactions. As they make an appropriate contribution to the group (a behavior indicated on one of the cards), they can turn the cards over and try another behavior.

3. Assignment of appropriate buddies to support the students may be one way to enable students to participate in activities without demanding supervision from the teacher. Again, a cross-age grouping arrangement with a classroom of older students can provide a teacher with responsible helpers during guided reading time. Older students may benefit from keeping a journal to record their plans for working with the students and their reflections on how well their work sessions went. It actually might be helpful for the classroom teacher to review the notes taken during times when he or she can't directly supervise a student with special needs.

4. It is critical to establish a smooth working arrangement with other educators in order to provide support services for the student with identified exceptional needs. The ability and willingness to work with these colleagues can lead to important support in the regular classroom during guided reading times when supervised activity is needed but cannot be provided by the teacher.

5. For students whose needs have not been formally identified as exceptional—other conditions like ADD and ADHD—center-based activity actually can be helpful because it allows them to move around and/or work with more physical/tactile activities. For easily distracted students, some teachers have discovered that the use of earphones helps to minimize distractions and keeps them more focused when they have to work independently in an environment buzzing with activity. It is important to create spaces where a student can go to avoid interfering distractions without isolating him or her from teacher supervision.

6. One advantage that can be built into center-based instruction is that students with identified exceptional needs can be given more choices, either a wider range of activities or a lot of individual inquiry projects. Therefore there is a greater likelihood of finding an activity that will engage a student than if all students are asked to complete the same activity. Building in choice allows all students to find at least one activity at which they can experience success, thus minimizing potential frustrations with whole-class assignments. Choice also removes limits on those students who have the interest and abilities to go way beyond basic expectations.

7. As we noted in Chapter 2, we need to make strategic decisions when grouping all students, and this is especially true for those with special needs. A mixed-achievement group can work well if an effort is made to be sure the cooperative task has the potential of involving all students; otherwise, stronger students may take over and those that need the practice the most may not get it (Matthews and Kesner, 2000). On the other hand, a similar-level achievement group may not provide enough positive models of academic and/or social behaviors for those students who need them the most. Some teachers have discovered that partnering students who have a wide gap in achievement level (proficient with novice) might not be as effective as partnering students with a narrower gap (proficient with partially proficient, or developing with novice). Pairing children who appear similar can be advantageous because each brings different strengths to the task at hand. Using their strengths, the students can help each other out with their areas of need.

Final Reminders

No matter what decisions are made about using quided reading, we need to state again that any instruction away from the teacher needs to be as powerful as instruction with the teacher. Like instruction with the teacher, it needs to be grounded in knowledge of the children—their reading and writing know-how and their degree of independence. Like instruction with the teacher, it needs to be sensitive to the external demands of standards, curricula, and assessments. Like instruction with the teacher, it needs to involve children in an unceasing cycle of self-improvement by continued engagement with print-rich activities. Like instruction with the teacher, children and adults need to see it as both accessible and purposeful. And, like instruction with the teacher, it needs to set children up for success so that they will see themselves as independent readers—the ultimate goal of guided reading. Just remember to . . .

- Avoid busy work.
- Keep activities focused on literacy.
- Make sure to provide actual practice with the real thing rather than projects that lead students away from reading and writing.
- Keep it simple.
- Keep it manageable!

References

Alexander, P. A. 1996. "The Past, Present, and Future of Knowledge Research: A Re-examination of the Role of Knowledge in Learning and Instructing." *Educational Psychologist* 31: 89–92.

Alexander, P. A., and T. L. Jetton. 2000. "Learning From Text: A Multidimensional and Developmental Perspective." In *Handbook of Reading Research, Volume III*, ed. M. L. Kamil, P. B. Mosenthal, P. D. Pearson, R. Barr, 285–310. Mahwah, NJ: Erlbaum.

Allington, R. 2001. *What Really Matters for Struggling Readers: Designing Research-based Programs*. New York: Addison-Wesley.

Allington, R., and P. Cunningham. 1996. *Schools That Work*. New York: HarperCollins.

Almasi, J. F., M. G. McKeown, and I. L. Beck. 1996. "The Return of Engaged Reading in Classroom Discussions of Literature." *Journal of Literary Research* 28: 107–46.

Bamford, R., and J. Kristo. 1998. *Making Facts Come Alive: Choosing Quality Nonfiction Literature, K–8*. Norwood, MA: Christopher-Gordon.

Barr, R. 1995. "What Research Says About Grouping in the Past and Present and What It Suggests for the Future." In *Flexible Grouping for Literacy in the Elementary Grades*, ed. M. Rodenrich and L. McKay. Needham Heights, MA: Longwood.

Barrera, R., V. Thompson, and M. Dressman. 1997. *Kaleidoscope, 2d ed.* Urbana, IL: National Council of Teachers of English.

Betts, E. 1946. *Foundations of Reading Instruction*. New York: American Book Company.

Boyle, O., and S. Peregoy. 1998. "Literary Scaffolds: Strategies for First- and Second-Language Readers and Writers." In *Literary Instruction for Culturally and Linguistically Diverse Students*, ed. M. Opitz (pp. 150–156). Newark, DE: International Reading Association.

Brophy, J. 1987. "Synthesis of Research on Strategies for Motivating Students to Learn." *Educational Leadership* 54: 40–45.

Brown, A., and A. Palinscar. 1982. "Inducing Strategic Learning from Texts by Means of Informed Self-Control Training." *Topics in Learning Disabilities* 2(1): 1–17.

Brown, K. 1999/2000. "What Kind of Text—For Whom and When? Textual Scaffolding for Beginning Readers." *The Reading Teacher* 53: 292–307.

Buehl, D. 2001. *Classroom Strategies for Interactive Learning*. 2d ed. Newark, DE: International Reading Association.

Buss, K., and L. Karnowski. 2000. *Reading and Writing Literary Genres*. Newark, DE: International Reading Association.

Caldwell, J., and M. Ford. 1996. *Where Have All the Bluebirds Gone? Transforming Ability-Based Reading Classrooms*. Schofield, WI: Wisconsin State Reading Association.

Calkins, L. 2000. *The Art of Teaching Reading*. New York: Addison-Wesley.

Camp, D. 2000. "It Takes Two; Teaching with Twin Texts of Fact and Fiction." *The Reading Teacher* 53: 400–408.

Children's Choices. 1995. *More Kids' Favorite Books*. Newark, DE: International Reading Association.

Clay, M. 1991a. *Becoming Literate: The Construction of Inner Control*. Portsmouth, NH: Heinemann.

Clay, M. 1991b. "Introducing a New Storybook to Young Readers." *The Reading Teacher* 45: 264–273.

Clay, M. 1993. *An Observational Survey of Early Literary Achievement*. Portsmouth, NH: Heinemann.

Cunningham, P., D. Hall, and J. Cunningham. 2000. *Guided Reading the Four Blocks Way*. Greensboro, NC: Carson-Dellosa.

Davey, B. 1983. "Think Aloud—Modeling the Cognitive Processes of Reading Comprehension." *Journal of Reading* 27: 44–47.

DeFord, D., C. Lyons, and G. Pinnell. 1991. *Bridges to Literacy: Learning from Reading Recovery*. Portsmouth, NH: Heinemann.

Dewey, J. 1938. *Experience and Education*. New York: Macmillan.

Donoghue, M. 2001. *Using Literature Activities to Teach Content Areas to Emergent Readers*. Boston: Allyn and Bacon.

Fountas, I., and G. S. Pinnell. 1996. *Guided Reading*. Portsmouth, NH: Heinemann.

Gambrell, L. 1996. "Creating Classroom Cultures That Foster Reading Motivation." *The Reading Teacher* 50: 14–25.

Gambrell, L. B., and J. F. Almasi, eds. 1996. *Lively Discussions! Fostering Engaged Reading*. Newark, DE: International Reading Association.

Gates, A. 1928. *New Methods in Primary Reading*. New York: Teachers' College Press.

Gill, S. R. 2000. "Reading with Amy: Teaching and Learning Through Reading Conferences." *The Reading Teacher* 53: 500–509.

Goforth, Frances. 1998. *Literature and the Learner*. Belmont, CA: Wadsworth.

Goldman, S. R., and J. A. Rakestraw Jr. 2000. "Structural Aspects of Constructing Meaning from Text." In *Handbook of Reading Research, Volume III*, ed. M. L. Kamil, P. B. Mosenthal, P. D. Pearson, and R. Barr, 311–35. Mahwah, NJ: Erlbaum.

Goodman, Y., and A. Marek. 1996. *Retrospective Miscue Analysis: Revaluing Readers and Reading*. New York: R. C. Owens.

Griffin, M. 2001. "Social Contexts of Beginning Reading." *Language Arts* 78: 371–78.

Gunning, T. 1998. *Best Books for Beginning Readers.* Boston: Allyn and Bacon.

Harris, V. ed. 1997. *Using Multicultural Literature in the K–8 Classroom.* Norwood, MA: Christopher-Gordon.

Harris-Helm, J., and L. Katz. 2001. *Young Investigators: The Project Approach in the Early Years.* New York: Teachers' College Press.

Harvey, S. 1998. *Nonfiction Matters: Reading, Writing, and Research in Grades 3–8.* York, ME: Stenhouse.

Heard, G. 1998. *Awakening the Heart: Exploring Poetry in Elementary and Middle School.* Portsmouth, NH: Heinemann.

Hearn, B. 1990. *Choosing Books for Children: A Commonsense Guide.* New York: Delacorte.

Kobrin, B. 1995. *Eyeopeners II: Children's Books to Answer Children's Questions About the World Around Them.* New York: Scholastic.

Krashen, S. 1993. *The Power of Reading: Insights from the Research.* Englewood, CO: Libraries Unlimited.

Leslie, L., and M. Jett-Simpson. 1997. *Authentic Literacy Assessment: An Ecological Approach.* New York: Addison Wesley Longman.

Loban, W. 1976. *Language Development: Kindergarten through Grade Twelve.* Research report #18. Final report. Urbana, IL: National Council of Teachers of English.

Matthews, M., and J. Kesner. 2000. "The Silencing of Sammy: One Struggling Reader Learning with His Peers." *The Reading Teachre* 53: 382–90.

McNeil, J. 1987. *Reading Comprehension: New Directions for Classroom Practice, 2d ed.* Glenview, IL: Scott-Foresman.

Mesmer, H. A. 1999. "Scaffolding a Crucial Transition Using Text with Some Decodability." *The Reading Teacher* 53: 130–42.

Mooney, M. 1995. "Guided Reading: The Reader in Control." *Teaching K–8,* 25(5): 54–58.

Mooney, M. 1990. *Reading To, With, and By Students.* Katonah, NY: R. C. Owen.

Muth, K. D., ed. 1989. *Children's Comprehension of Text.* Newark, DE: International Reading Association.

Nagel, G. 2001. *Effective Grouping for Literacy Instruction.* Boston: Allyn and Bacon.

Olivares, R. 1993. *Using Newspapers to Teach ESL Learners.* Newark, DE: International Reading Association.

Opitz, M. 1998. "Text Sets: One Way to Flex Your Grouping—in First Grade, Too!" *The Reading Teacher* 51: 622–24.

Opitz, M. 1998. *Flexible Grouping in Reading: Practical Ways to Help All Students Become Better Readers.* New York: Scholastic.

Opitz, M. 1995. *Getting the Most from Predictable Books.* New York: Scholastic.

Paris, S. 1983. *Metacognition and Reading Comprehension Skills.* (Final Report for the National Institute of Education.) Washington, D.C.: ERIC Document Reproduction Service, No. Ed 236 5700.

Petersen, B. 1991. "Selecting Books for Beginning Readers" in D. DeFord, C. Lyons, G. Pinnell, eds. *Bridges to Literacy.* Portsmouth, NH: Heinemann.

Pressley, M. 1998. *Reading Instruction that Works: The Case for Balanced Reading Instruction.* New York: Guilford Press.

Raphael, T. 1982. "Question-Answering Strategies for Children." *The Reading Teacher* 36: 186–190.

Reed, J. H., and D. L. Schallert. 1993. "The Nature of Involvement in Academic Discourse." *Journal of Educational Psychology* 85: 253–66.

Renzulli, J. 1998. "A Rising Tide Lifts All Ships: Developing the Gifts and Talents of All Students." *Phi Delta Kappan* 80: 104–11.

Richeck, M. A., and B. K. McTague. 1988. "The 'Curious George' Strategy for Students with Reading Problems." *The Reading Teacher* 42: 220–26.

Routman, R. 2000. *Conversations: Stategies for Teaching, Learning, and Evaluating.* Portsmouth, NH: Heinemann.

Smith, J., and W. Elley. 1994. *Learning to Read in New Zealand.* Katonah, NY: R. C. Owens.

Snow, C., M. Burns, and P. Griffin. 1998. *Preventing Reading Difficulties in Young Children.* Washington, D.C.: National Academy Press.

Stoll, D., ed. 1997. *Magazines for Kids and Teens, Revised ed.* Glassboro, NJ: Educational Press Association of America; Newark, DE: International Reading Association.

Sweeney, J. 1993. *Teaching Poetry: Yes You Can!* New York: Scholastic.

Teale, W. H., and J. Yokota. 2000. "Beginning Reading and Writing: Perspectives on Instruction." In *Beginning Reading and Writing,* ed. D. Strickland and L. Morrow, 3–21. Newark, DE: International Reading Association.

Thogmartin, M. B. 1998. *Teach a Child to Read with Children's Books, 2d ed.* Bloomington, IN: Educational Resource Information Center.

Traill, L. 1993. *Highlight My Strengths: Assessment and Evaluation of Literacy Learning.* Crystal Lake, IL: Rigby.

Watson, D. 1997. "Beyond Decodable Texts: Supportive and Workable Literature." *Language Arts* 74(8): 635–43.

Wertsch, J. V. 1985. *Vygotsky and the Societal Formation of Mind.* Cambridge, MA: Harvard University Press.

Wilkinson, L. C., and E. R. Silliman. 2000. "Classroom Language and Literacy Learning." In *Handbook of Reading Research, Volume III,* ed. M. L. Kamil, P. B. Mosenthal, P. D. Pearson, and R. Barr, 337–60. Mahwah, NJ: Erlbaum.

Winebrenner, S. 2001. *Teaching Gifted Kids in the Regular Classroom: Strategies and Techniques Every Teacher Can Use to Meet the Academic Needs of the Gifted and Talented.* Minneapolis: Free Spirit Publishing.

Wong, B., and W. Jones. 1982. "Increasing Metacomprehension in Learning Disabled and Normally Achieving Students Through Self-Questioning Training." *Learning Disability Quarterly* 5: 228–39.

Yinger, R. J., and M. S. Hendricks-Lee. 1993. "An Ecological Conception of Teaching." *Learning and Individual Differences* 4: 269–81.

Yopp, R. H., and H. K. Yopp. 2000. "Sharing Informational Text with Young Children." *The Reading Teacher* 53: 410–23.

Children's Books Cited

Brink, C. *Caddie Woodlawn*. 1997. New York: Aladdin (0689815212).

Cleary, B. 1992. *Ramona Quimby, Age 8*. New York: Camelot (030709562).

Cole, R. *The Story of Ruby Bridges*. New York: Scholastic. (0590572814).

Creech, S. 1994. *Walk Two Moons*. New York: HarperTrophy. 0064405176.

Curtis, C. 1999. *Bud, Not Buddy*. New York: Delacorte (0385323069).

Dakos, K. 1995. *If You're Not Here, Please Raise Your Hand: Poems About School*. New York: Aladdin (0680801165).

Dorris M. 1999. *Sees Behind Trees*. New York: Hyperion (0786813571).

Dorros, A. 1997. *A Tree Is Growing*. New York: Scholastic (0590453009).

Ehlert, L. 1991. *Red Leaf, Yellow Leaf*. New York: Harcourt Brace (0152661972).

Fleischman, P. 1989. *Joyful Noise: Poems for Two Voices*. New York: HarperCollins (0064460932).

Florian, D. 1996. *On the Wing: Bird Poems and Paintings*. New York: Harcourt Brace (0152004971).

Ganeri, G. 1995. *Animals in Disguise*. New York: Little Simon (0689802641).

Greenburg, D. 1999. *The Boy Who Cried Big Foot (Zack Files)*. New York: Grosset and Dunlap (0448420414).

Hall, Z. 2000. *Fall Leaves Fall*. New York: Scholastic (0590100793).

Hest, A. 1997. *When Jessie Came Across the Sea*. Cambridge, MA: Candlewick (073600946).

Lobel, A. 1979. *Frog and Toad Are Friends*. New York: HarperCollins (0064440206).

Lowry, L. 1993. *The Giver*. Boston: Houghton Mifflin (0395645662).

Martin, B. 1991. *Polar Bear, Polar Bear, What Do You Hear?* New York: Holt (0805017593).

Meddaugh, S. 1992. *Martha Speaks*. Boston: Houghton Mifflin (0395633133).

Mills, C. 1997. *Gus and Grandpa*. New York: Farrar, Straus, & Giroux (0374328242).

Morris, A. 1998. *Work*. New York: Lothrop (0688148662).

Naylor, P. 2000. *Shiloh*. New York: Aladdin (0689835825).

Neitzel, S. 1989. *The Jacket I Wear in the Snow*. New York: Mulberry (0688080286).

Nikoli-Lisa, W. 1997. *America: My Land, Your Land, Our Land*. New York: Lee and Low (1880000377).

Paulsen, G. 1995. *Dancing Carl*. New York: Aladdin (0689804105).

Reilly-Giff, P. 1988. *Meet the Polk Street Kids (Polk Street Kids Series)*. New York: Doubleday (0440443857).

Rowling, J. K. 1998. *Harry Potter and the Sorcerer's Stone* (first book of series). New York: Scholastic (0590353403).

Rose, D. 2000. *Into the A, B, Sea*. New York: Scholastic (0439096960).

Rylant, C. 1996. *An Angel for Solemn Singer*. New York: Orchard (0531070824).

Rylant, C. 1996. *Henry and Mudge*. New York: Aladdin (0689810059).

Rylant, C. 1993. *Missing May*. New York: Yearling (0440408652).

Schnur, S. 1997. *Autumn: An Alphabet Acrostic*. New York: Clarion (0395770432).

Silverstein, S. *Spaghetti*. 1974. In *Where the Sidewalk Ends*. New York: HarperCollins (006025662.)

Taylor, M. 1987. *The Gold Cadillac*. New York: Bantam (0553157655).

Tildes, P. 2000. *Animals in Camouflage*. New York: Charlesbridge (0881061344).

Tildes, P. 1996. *Calico Picks a Puppy*. New York: Charlesbridge (0881068918).

Tildes, P. 1995. *Counting on Calico*. New York: Charlesbridge (0881068632).

USA Today. "What's a Nurtra? A Really Nasty 'Beast.'"

Warner, G. 1989. *Boxcar Children #1*. New YorK: Whitman (0807508527).

Wilder, L. I. 1971. *Little House in the Big Woods*. New York: HarperTrophy (0064400018).

Williams, S. 1990. *I Went Walking*. New York: Harcourt Brace (0152380116).

Wood, N. 1997. *The Serpent's Tongue: Prose, Poetry, and Art of the New Mexico Pueblos*. New York: Dutton (0525462945).

APPENDIX A

Assessment Procedures and Protocol Forms

Running Record

Administering

1. Choose a text or passage.

2. Make copies of both the Running Record form and the Running Record Summary form (see pages 123–24).

3. Assess children individually. Begin by saying something such as this: "I would like to listen to you read this book. While you are reading, I am going to take some notes so that I can remember how well you read." Sit next to the child so that you can watch his or her behaviors rather than the reverse!

4. Have the children read the book while you record the reading on the Running Record form (page 123). Use the following notations:

   - Make a check for each word read as shown in the book.
   - Write and circle any word that is omitted.
   - Add a caret for any word that the child inserts and write the word.
   - Write and draw a line through any word that is substituted and write what the child said in its place.
   - If the child repeats, draw an arrow to indicate where the child went back to reread.
   - Write SC when the child self-corrects.

5. To check comprehension, have the child do a retelling. See below for a sample procedure and page 127 for a suggested form.

Scoring

1. Write M, S, V for each error and self-correction. Remember that a self-correction is not counted as an error. Likewise, a repetition is not counted as an error.

2. Read the sentence up to where each error was made and ask yourself these questions:

   - Does it make sense? If so, circle the M.
   - Does it sound right? If so, circle the S.
   - Does it look like the actual word in the text? If so, circle the V.

3. For each self-correction, you need to ask yourself what made the reader go back to self-correct. Ask yourself these questions:

   - Did the child self-correct because meaning was disrupted? If so, circle the M.
   - Did the child self-correct because it didn't sound right? If so, circle the S.
   - Did the child self-correct because the word didn't look like the one shown in the text? If so, circle the V.

4. Calculate the accuracy rate and the self-correction rate using the formula shown on the Running Record Summary form (page 124).

5. Record additional observations on the Running Record Summary form (page 124).

6. Use the results to plan for meaningful instruction.

Modified Miscue Analysis

Administering

1. Choose a text that contains at least 100 words.

2. Make a copy for the child to read from and have another for yourself. You will make your markings on this copy.

3. Assess children individually. Begin by saying something such as this:
   "I would like to listen to you read this book. While you are reading, I am going to take some notes so that I can remember how well you read." Sit next to the child so that you can watch his or her behaviors rather than the reverse!

4. As the child reads, make the following notations on your copy of the passage:
   - Circle any word that the child omits.
   - Add a caret for any word that the child inserts and write the inserted word.
   - Draw a line through any word that is substituted. Write the substituted word.
   - Write a C on top of the word if the child self-corrects.
   - Note repetitions by writing R and drawing a line back to where the child repeats.

5. To check comprehension, have the child do a retelling. See below for a sample procedure and page 127 for a suggested form.

Scoring

1. Using the Modified Miscue Analysis Form shown on page 125, analyze the child's miscues. Here's how:
   - Write each miscue in the "student" column and the actual text in the "text" column. Remember that self-corrections and repetitions are not counted as miscues.
   - For each miscue, ask the three questions shown on the form. If the answer is yes, circle the appropriate letter.

2. Use this analysis and the markings on the passage to complete the Summary of Observation form shown on page 126.

3. Based on your analysis, determine what you think the child needs to learn and design instruction accordingly.

Retelling

Administering

1. Make a copy of the Retelling form shown on page 127 or use it to design one of your own. In either case, read the form carefully so that you will know exactly what to listen for once the retelling begins.

2. Select a text for the child to read.

4. Ask the student to read the text.

5. Once the child has finished reading, have him or her do a retell. Say something such as, "Tell me everything you can remember about this passage. Pretend you are telling it to a person who has not read it."

6. As the student retells, use the form to record what you hear. You can use prompts such as "What comes next?" or "Anything else?"

Scoring

1. Look at your markings.

2. Make any notes in the "Interpretation" section at the bottom of the form.

3. Use this analysis when planning instruction.

Primary Reading Survey

Administering

1. Make copies of the Primary Reading Survey form shown on page 128.

2. Either individually or as a group, have students complete the survey with your guidance. Read each statement and give time for students to place a check under the face that best represents how they feel about the statement.

Scoring

1. Take a look at how the children marked the different statements. A majority of checks under the face with the big smile indicates a positive attitude about reading, whereas several checks under the sad face suggests the opposite.

Reading Attitude Survey for Grades 3–6

Administering

1. Make copies of the Reading Attitude Survey form shown on page 129 for each student.

2. Tell students that you would like to know something about how they feel about reading, saying something such as, "I am going to read each statement on the form. Circle the letter that best tells how you feel about the statement."

3. Read each statement, pausing long enough for students to make their choice.

Scoring

1. Score the surveys using the following code:
   SA = 1; A = 2; U = 3; D = 4; SD = 5

2. Add the points for positive and negative statements. Items 1, 3, 4, 6, 8, 9, 11, 12, 13, 16, 17, and 20 reflect negative attitudes. Items 2, 5, 7, 10, 14, 15, 18, and 19 reflect positive attitudes.

3. Determine who has positive and negative attitudes about reading. Scores above 60 indicate a positive attitude toward reading.

Student Interview

Administering

1. Make a copy of the Student Interview guide shown on page 130 for each student.

2. Individually interview each student. These interviews should take no more than 10 minutes. Use the form to record what the child tells you.

3. Because this is an unstructured interview, the questions can be asked in any order. Also note that some questions may need to be reworded.

Scoring

1. Take a look at the first three questions. These are designed to elicit students' perceptions of reading. Do students' answers focus on reading as a meaning-making activity? Do their answers focus on calling words? Do they focus on something other than understanding or word calling?

2. Take a look at questions 4 through 7. These are designed to elicit strategies used in reading. Do students' responses indicate limited strategies?

3. Use the results when planning instruction.

Interest Inventory

Administering

1. Make a copy of the Interest Inventory form shown on page 131 for each student.

2. Provide time for students to complete the form. This can be done as a whole class or during brief individual conferences. You may also decide that you need to read this to students and write what they tell you in the appropriate spaces on the form.

Scoring

1. Tally the results on a matrix. List students' names down the left and reading interests across the top. Place a check in the space to indicate those topics that are of interest to each child.

2. Use the chart to select texts for your classroom.

Multidimensional Fluency Scale

Administering

1. Select a passage.
2. Make a copy of the passage for the students to read from and another for you to write on when the child is reading.
3. Read through the Multidementional Fluency Scale shown on page 132 to become familiar with what you will be rating.
4. Show the passage to the student and allow him or her time to read it silently once or twice.
5. Ask the student to read the passage orally. While reading, mark phrasing on your copy using slashes between the words to show how the child is chunking the text.
6. Have the child do a retelling (see above and page 127 for a sample form).

Scoring

1. Rate the student on the fluency scale by circling the number in front of the description that best describes how the student read.
2. Attach the passage you marked to the fluency scale.
3. Interpret results and design instruction accordingly.

Print Concepts

Administering

1. Choose a book that is relatively short.
2. Make the necessary copies of the Print Concepts form shown on page 133.
3. Read through the form to become familiar with what you will be asking and to make sure the book you will be using has the appropriate examples as noted on the form.
4. Individually, complete the assessment following the directions stated on the form (page 133).

Scoring

1. Look at the responses that a given child provided.
2. Record your observations on the Summary of Print Concepts form on page 134.
3. Use the results to plan instruction.

Name _____ Date _____

RUNNING RECORD

Title of Book _____ Author _____

Page	Reading Performance	Miscues M S V	Self-Corrects M S V
		TOTALS	

M = Meaning Cue   S = Structure Cue   V = Visual Cue

Originally published in *Flexible Grouping in Reading* by Michael F. Opitz (Scholastic Professional Books, 1998).
Copyright © Michael F. Opitz.

Name _____ Date _____

RUNNING RECORD SUMMARY

Title of Book _____ Author _____

Summary of Reading Performance

Total # of Words _____   Total # of Miscues _____   % of Accuracy _____

Reading Level (Circle the one that matches the % of accuracy.)

95%–100% = Independent   90–94% = Instructional   89% or lower = Frustration

Total # of Self-Corrections _____   Self-Correction rate 1: _____

NOTE: Self-correction rates of 1:3, 1:4, or 1:5 are good. Each ratio shows that the reader is attending to discrepancies when reading.

- -

Summary of Observation

1. What did the reader do when unknown words were encountered?

   _____ made an attempt

   The reader made an attempt in these ways:

   _____ asked for help   _____ looked at pictures

   _____ used letter/sound knowledge   _____ used meaning

   _____ used structure (syntax)   _____ tried again

   _____ skipped it and continued reading   _____ looked at another source

2. How often did the reader attempt to self-correct when meaning was not maintained?

   (Circle one)   always   frequently   sometimes   seldom   never

3. When the reader did self-correct, which cues were used? (✔all that apply.)

   _____ letter/sound knowledge (visual)   _____ meaning   _____ syntax (structure)

Calculating Accuracy Rate

1. Subtract the total number of miscues from the total number of words in the text to determine the number of words that were correctly read.

2. Divide the number of words correctly read by the number of words in the passage to determine % of accuracy.

   EXAMPLE: 58 total words – 12 miscues = 46 words read correctly

   46 words read correctly ÷ 58 total words = 79% accuracy

Calculating Self-Correction Rate

Use this formula: $\dfrac{\text{self-correction} + \text{miscues}}{\text{self-corrections}} = 1:\underline{\quad}$

Originally published in *Flexible Grouping in Reading* by Michael F. Opitz (Scholastic Professional Books, 1998).
Copyright © Michael F. Opitz. Based on Clay, 1993, and Morrison, 1994; adapted by M. Opitz.

MODIFIED MISCUE ANALYSIS FORM

Reader's Name _____ Grade _____

Title and Pages _____ Date _____

Three important questions to ask for each miscue:
 M = meaning: Does the miscue make sense?
 S = structure: Does the sentence sound right?
 V = visual: Does the miscue resemble the printed word?

Student	Text	Cues Used
		M S V
		M S V
		M S V
		M S V
		M S V
		M S V
		M S V
		M S V
		M S V
		M S V
		M S V
		M S V
		M S V
		M S V
		M S V
		M S V
		M S V

From *Good-Bye Round Robin* by M. F. Opitz & T. V. Rasinski, Portsmouth, NH: Heinemann. Adapted from Adele Fiderer (1995). Practical Assessments for Literature-Based Reading Classrooms. New York: Scholastic Professional Books.

MODIFIED MISCUE ANALYSIS:
SUMMARY OF OBSERVATIONS

1. What did the reader do when unknown words were encountered? (Check all that apply.)

    _____ made an attempt in these ways:

    _____ used meaning cues   _____ used structure cues   _____ used letter/sound cues

    _____ made repeated tries   _____ used pictures   _____ skipped it and read on

    _____ used memory   _____ looked at another source

    _____ other: _____

    _____ made no attempt   _____ asked for help   _____ waited for teacher help

2. Which cues did the reader use most often? _____

    _____

3. How often did the reader attempt to self-correct when meaning was not maintained?

    (Circe one)   always   sometimes   seldom   never

    Comments: _____

4. How often did the reader make repetitions?

    (Circe one)   always   sometimes   seldom   never

    Comments: _____

5. Did the reader read fluently? _____ mostly   _____ somewhat   _____ little

    Comments: _____

6. Did the reader attend to punctuation? _____ mostly   _____ somewhat   _____ little

    Comments: _____

Comprehension

Retelling was (Circle one):   outstanding   adequate   inadequate

Comments: _____

_____

Other observations: _____

_____

From *Good-Bye Round Robin* by M. F. Opitz & T. V. Rasinski, Portsmouth, NH: Heinemann. Adapted from Adele Fiderer (1995). *Practical Assessments for Literature-Based Reading Classrooms.* New York: Scholastic Professional Books.

Name _____

RETELLING

Directions: Indicate with a check the extent to which the reader's retelling includes or provides evidence of the following information.

Retelling	None	Low	Moderate	High
1. Includes information directly stated in text.				
2. Includes information inferred directly or indirectly from text.				
3. Includes what is important to remember from text.				
4. Provides relevant content and concepts.				
5. Indicates attempt to connect background knowledge to text information.				
6. Indicated attempt to make summary statements or generalizations based on text that can be applied to the real world.				
7. Indicated highly individualistic and creative impressions of or reactions to the real world.				
8. Indicates effective involvement with the text.				
9. Demonstrates appropriate use of language (vocabulary, sentence structure, language conventions).				
10. Indicates ability to organize or compose the retelling.				
11. Demonstrates sense of audience or purpose.				
12. Indicates control of the mechanics of speaking or writing.				

Interpretation: Items 1–4 indicate the reader's comprehension of textual information; items 5–8 indicate metacognitive awareness, strategy use, and involvement with text; items 9–12 indicate facility with language and language development.

Originally published in *Flexible Grouping in Reading* by Michael F. Opitz (Scholastic Professional Books, 1998).
Copyright © Michael F. Opitz. Source: Adapted from Pi A. Irwin and Judy N. Mitchell.

Name _____

PRIMARY READING SURVEY

How do you feel when:	🙂	😐	☹️
1. your teacher reads a story to you?			
2. your class has reading time?			
3. you can read with a friend?			
4. you read out loud to your teacher?			
5. you read out loud to someone at home?			
6. someone reads to you at home?			
7. someone gives you a book for a present?			
8. you read a book to yourself at home?			
How do you think:			
9. your teacher feels when you read out loud?			
10. your family feels when you read out loud?			

**How do you feel about how well you can read?
Make this face look the way you feel.**

Originally published in *Flexible Grouping in Reading* by Michael F. Opitz (Scholastic Professional Books, 1998).
Copyright © Michael F. Opitz. Adapted from *Practical Assessments for Literature-Based Reading Classrooms* by Adele
Fiderer, Scholastic Professional Books, 1995.

Name _____

READING ATTITUDE SURVEY FOR GRADES 3 AND UP

Directions: The 20 statements that follow will be read to you. After each statement is read, circle the letter that best describes how you feel about that statement. Your answers will not be graded because there are no right answers. Your feeling about each statement is what's important.

SA = Strongly Agree   A = Agree   U = Undecided
D = Disagree   SD = Strongly Disagree

SA A U D SD   **1.** Reading is for learning but not for enjoyment.

SA A U D SD   **2.** Money spent on books is well spent.

SA A U D SD   **3.** There is nothing to be gained by reading books.

SA A U D SD   **4.** Books are a bore.

SA A U D SD   **5.** Reading is a good way to spend spare time.

SA A U D SD   **6.** Sharing books in class is a waste of time.

SA A U D SD   **7.** Reading turns me on.

SA A U D SD   **8.** Reading is only for students seeking good grades.

SA A U D SD   **9.** Books aren't usually good enough to finish.

SA A U D SD   **10.** Reading is rewarding to me.

SA A U D SD   **11.** Reading becomes boring after about an hour.

SA A U D SD   **12.** Most books are too long and dull.

SA A U D SD   **13.** Free reading doesn't teach anything.

SA A U D SD   **14.** There should be more time for free reading during the school day.

SA A U D SD   **15.** There are many books I hope to read.

SA A U D SD   **16.** Books should not be read except for class requirements.

SA A U D SD   **17.** Reading is something I can do without.

SA A U D SD   **18.** A certain amount of summer vacation should be set aside for reading.

SA A U D SD   **19.** Books make good presents.

SA A U D SD   **20.** Reading is dull.

Originally published in *Flexible Grouping in Reading* by Michael F. Opitz (Scholastic Professional Books, 1998). Copyright © Michael F. Opitz. From *Improving Reading: Strategies & Reading,* Third Edition by Jerry L. Johns and Susan Davis Lenski. Copyright © 1994, 1997, 2001 Kendall/Hunt Publishing Company. Used with permission.

Name _____

Student Interview

1. What is the most important thing about reading?

   _____

   _____

2. When you are reading, what are you trying to do?

   _____

   _____

3. What is reading?

   _____

   _____

4. When you come to a word you don't know, what do you do?

   _____

   _____

5. Do you think it is important to read every word correctly? Why? Why not?

   _____

   _____

6. What makes a person a good reader?

   _____

   _____

7. Do you think good readers ever come to a word they don't know? If yes, what do you think they do?

   _____

   _____

Originally published in *Flexible Grouping in Reading* by Michael F. Opitz (Scholastic Professional Books, 1998).
Copyright © Michael F. Opitz.

Name _____ Date _____

INTEREST INVENTORY

Please ✓ the right spaces to help me get to know you!

1. Do you like to read?

   _____ yes   _____ sometimes   _____ no

2. What kind of books do you like to read? (✓ as many as you want!)

   _____ animal   _____ science   _____ true

   _____ make-believe   _____ about people   _____ science fiction

   _____ mysteries   _____ poetry   _____ funny

   _____ series   _____ myths   _____ folktales

   _____ plays   _____ riddles/jokes   _____ books with pictures

   _____ scary stories   _____ books that tell how to make things

   _____ sports

3. Who is your favorite author? _____

4. What is your favorite book? _____

5. What book would you like to read? _____

6. What magazines do you like to read? _____

   _____

7. Which do you like best?

   _____ hardcover books   _____ softcover books

   Why? _____

   _____

8. What helps you to choose a book to read?

   _____

   _____

   _____

Originally published in *Flexible Grouping in Reading* by Michael F. Opitz (Scholastic Professional Books, 1998).
Copyright © Michael F. Opitz.

MULTIDIMENSIONAL FLUENCY SCALE

Student's name: _____ Date _____

Text selection: _____

Directions: Use the scale in all three areas to rate reader fluency. Circle the number in each category that best corresponds to your observations.

Phrasing

1   Monotonic with little sense of phrase boundaries; frequent word-by-word reading.

2   Frequent two- and three-word phrases, giving the impression of choppy reading; improper stress and intonation that fails to mark ends of sentences and clauses.

3   Mixture of run-ons, midsentence pauses for breath, and possibly some choppiness; reasonable stress / intonation.

4   Generally well-phrased, mostly in clause and sentence units with adequate attention to expression.

Smoothness

1   Frequent extended pauses, hesitations, false starts, sound-outs, repetitions, and/or multiple attempts.

2   Several "rough spots" in text where extended pauses hesitations, and so on, are more frequent and disruptive.

3   Occasional breaks in smoothness caused by difficulties with specific words and/or structures.

4   Generally smooth reading with some breaks, but word and structure difficulties are resolved quickly, usually through self-correction.

Pace

1   Slow and laborious

2   Moderately slow

3   Uneven mixture of fast and slow reading

4   Consistently conversational

From *Good-Bye Round Robin* by M. F. Opitz & T. V. Rasinski. Portsmouth, NH: Heinemann. Adapted by J. Zutell and T. Rasinski, 1991.

Name _____ Date _____

PRINT CONCEPTS

Directions: Using the book that you have selected, give the following prompts to encourage the child to interact with it. Read the story aloud as you proceed. Place a ✓ next to each item answered correctly.

Prompt	Response (✓ = correct)	Print Concept
1. Hand the child the book upside down, spine first, saying something like: "Show me the front of this book." Then read the title to the child.		layout of book
2. Say: "I would like to begin reading the story, but I need your help. Please open the book and point to the exact spot where I should begin reading."		print conveys message
3. Stay on the same page and say: "Point to where I need to start reading."		directionality: where to begin
4. Say: "Point to where I should go after I start reading."		directionality: left-to-right progression
5. Say: "Point to where I go next." Read the pair of pages.		directionality: return sweep
6. Turn the page and say: "Point to where I should begin reading on this page. Now point to where I should end." Read the page.		terminology: beginning and end
7. Turn the page and say: "Point to the bottom of this page. Point to the top of it. Now point to the middle of it." Read the page.		terminology: top, bottom, middle
8. Using the same page, say: "Point to one word."		terminology: word
9. Again using the same page, say: "Point to one letter."		terminology: letter
10. Turn the page. Make sure that this page contains words that have corresponding upper-and lower-case letters. Read the pages. Then point to a capital letter and say: "Point to a little letter that is like this one."		matching lower- to uppercase letters
11. Turn the page and say: "Let's read these pages together. I'll read and you point." Read the pages.		speech to print match
12. Finish reading the book. Then turn back to a page that has the punctuation marks you want to assess. Point to the punctuation mark and say: "What is this? What is it for?"		punctuation: perod, question mark, quotation marks

Originally published in *Flexible Grouping in Reading* by Michael F. Opitz (Scholastic Professional Books, 1998).
Copyright © Michael F. Opitz.

Name _____ Date _____

SUMMARY OF PRINT CONCEPTS

Directions: Use this form to summarize your observations of print concepts.

Observations

The child demonstrates knowledge of the following print concepts (✔ the appropriate spaces)

_____ layout of books (item 1)

_____ print contains written message (item 2)

_____ directionality (items 3, 4, 5)

_____ terminology associated with reading (items 6, 7, 8, 9)

_____ uppercase letters (item 10)

_____ lowercase letters (item 10)

_____ speech to print match (item 11)

_____ punctuation (item 12)

Comments/Notes

_____

_____

_____

_____

_____

_____

_____

_____

_____

_____

_____

_____

_____

_____

_____

_____

_____

APPENDIX B

Selected Bibliography of Multilevel Texts

Title	Author	ISBN/ Version	Company/Year	Grade Level[1]
Air Show	Suen	0-8050-4952-5 Hardback	Holt/2001	1–3
Animals Black and White	Tildes	0-88106-959-0 Paperback	Charlesbridge/1996	1–2
Animals Brightly Colored	Tildes	0-88106-978-7 Paperback	Charlesbridge/1998	1–2
Animal Dads	Collard III	0-618-03299-1 Paperback	Holt/2001 Houghton Mifflin/1997	1–2
Bald Eagle	Morison	0-395-87328 Hardback	Houghton Mifflin/1998	2–4
The Baseball Counting Book	McGrath	0-88106-333-9 Paperback	Charlesbridge/1999	1–2
Beach Feet	Reiser	0-688-14400-4 Hardback	Greenwillow/1996	1–6[2]
Biggest, Strongest, Fastest	Jenkins	0-395-69701-8 Hardback	Tricknor & Fields (Houghton Mifflin)/1995	1–2
Blast Off! A Space Counting Book	Cole	0-88106-498-X Paperback	Charlesbridge/1994	1–3
Bridges Are to Cross	Sturges	0-399-23174-9 Hardback	Putnam/1998	1–3
Bugs for Lunch	Facklam	0-88106-272-3 Paperback	Charlesbridge/1999	1
Calico's Cousins: Cats from Around the World	Tildes	0-88106-649-4 Paperback	Charlesbridge/1999	2–4
Calico Picks a Puppy	Tildes	0-88106-891-8 Paperback	Charlesbridge/1996	1–2
California Here We Come!	Ryan	0-88106-880-2 Paperback	Charlesbridge/1997	3–5

[1] Grade at which several children should be able to read the easiest part of the text; grade at which most students will be interested in the content of the text.
[2] The book could be used to teach older students how to write footnotes.

Can We Save Them?	Dobson	0-88106-822-5	Charlesbridge/1997	1–5
Celebrate the 50 States	Leedy	0-8234-1431-0 Hardback	Holiday House/1999	3–6
Counting is for the Birds	Mazzola	0-88106-950-7 Paperback	Charlesbridge/1997	2–3
Counting on Calico	Tildes	0-88106-862-4 Paperback	Charlesbridge/1995	1–3
Crashed, Smashed, and Mashed: A Trip to Junkyard Heaven	Mitchell	1-58246-034-5	Tricyle/2001	1–5
Does a Kangaroo Have a Mother Too?	Carle	0-06-028768-3 Hardback	Harper/Collins/2000	1–2
Elephants Swim	Riley	0-395-73654-4 Hardback	Houghton Mifflin/1995	1–2
Fair Ball! 14 Great Stars From Baseball's Negro Leagues	Winter	0-590-39464-9 Hardback	Scholastic/1999	3–6
The Flag We Love	Ryan	0-88106-844-6	Charlesbridge/1996	2–5
Gathering: A Northwood's Counting Book	Bowen	0-395-98134-4 Paperback	Houghton Mifflin/1999	1–3
Gathering the Sun: An Alphabet in Spanish and English	Ada	0-688-13903-5 Hardback	Lothrop/1997	K–5
Gone Forever! An Alphabet of Extinct Animals	Markle	0-689-31961-4 Hardback	Atheneum/1998	3–6
Good Times with Teddy Bear	McQuade	0-8037-2076-9 Hardback	Dial/1997	K–1
Harvest Year	Peterson	1-56397-571-8 Hardback	Boyds Mills/1996	1–3
The Inside-Outside Book of Texas	Munro	1-58717-050-7 Hardback	SeaStar/2001	1–4
Jack's Garden	Cole	0-688-15283-X Paperback	Morrow/1995	1–3
Just Like You and Me	Miller	0-8037-2586-8 Hardback	Dial/2001	1–3
Kipper's A to Z: An Alphabet Adventure	Inkpen	0-15-202594-4 Hardback	Harcourt/2000	1–2
Lifetimes	Rice	1-883220-59-9 Paperback	Dawn/1997	1–6
Little Panda	Ryder	0-689-84310-0 Hardback	Simon & Schuster/2001	2–5
Making Animal Babies	Collard III	0-395-95317-0 Hardback	Houghton Mifflin/2000	3–6
Nature's Paintbrush	Stockdale	0-689-81081-4 Hardback	Simon & Schuster/1999	2–3

One Less Fish	Toft and Sheather	0-88106-323-1 Paperback	Charlesbridge/1998	K–3
One on a Web	Wadsworth	0-88106-973-6 Paperback	Charlesbridge/1997	1–3
One Tiger Growls	Wadsworth	0-88106-274-X Paperback	Charlesbridge/1999	1–3
The Sailor's Alphabet	McCurdy	0-395-84167-4 Hardback	Houghton Mifflin/1998	2–3
Say it Again	Cassie	0-88106-342-8 Paperback	Charlesbridge/2000	1–3
Sky Tree	Locker	0-06-024883-1 Hardback	HarperCollins/1995	3–6
Snowflake Bentley	Martin	0-395-86162-4 Hardback	Houghton Mifflin/ 1998	2–5
Spiders and Their Web Sites	Facklam	0-316-27329-5 Hardback	Little, Brown/2001	1–4
A Swim Through the Sea	Pratt	1-883220-04-1 Paperback	Dawn/1994	3–6
This is Our Earth	Benson	0-88106-838-1 Paperback	Charlesbridge/1994	1–3
Tools[3]	Morris	0-688-16165-0 Paperback	Morrow/1998	1–2
Touchdown Mars!	Wethered	0-399-23214-1	Putnam/2000	1–3
Tough Beginnings: How Baby Animals Survive	Singer	0-8050-6164-9 Hardback	Holt/2001	1–3
What a Viking!	Manning & Granstrom	91-29-64883-1 Hardback	R & S/2000	2–5
What You Never Knew About Tubs, Toilets, and Showers	Lauber	0-689-82420-3 Hardback	Simon & Schuster/2001	3–4
The Wolf Girls: An Unsolved Mystery from History	Yolen and Stemple	0-689-81080-6 Hardback	Simon & Schuster/2001	3–5
World Water Watch	Koch	0-688-16697-0 Paperback	Morrow/1993	2–3

[3] *Note:* There are several books in this series. All are formatted the same.

APPENDIX C

Blanks of Forms Described in Text

Group Grid

Student	Word Attempted	Miscue	Strategy Articulated	Strategy Used	Success	Cross-check	Insights

Names _____

The title of our book is _____

_____

The author of our book is _____

Beginning

Middle

End

Adapted from Juliet Sisnroy, Pueblo, CO

Characteristic Chart

Title	Setting	Plot	New Character

Planning Sheet for Team Reading

Team 1: **Section of Text:**	**Team 2:** **Section of Text:**
Team 3: **Section of Text:**	**Team 4:** **Section of Text:**
Teams 5: **Section of Text:**	**Team 6:** **Section of Text:**

Attribute Map

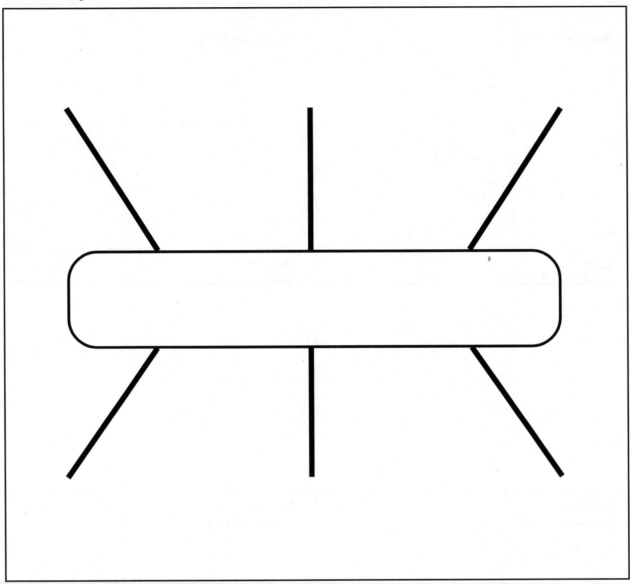

CHARACTER TO A "T"	
My thoughts	**What the author said**
Beginning:	
Middle:	
Near the end:	

Guided Reading Lesson Plan Form

Students

Considerations	Teaching Strategies
Purpose: ___ demonstration ___ intervention ___ shared response ___ combination *Focus:* Strategy: Literary element: Procedure/process:	**BEFORE**
Grouping: Type: ___ similar achievement ___ mixed achievement *Size:* small groups of _____ Assign by: need interest random large group *Texts:* ___ commercial ___ children's literature ___ other	**DURING**
Number: ___ single title ___ multiple titles Title(s): *Text Selection:* ___ student ___ teacher *Time:* ___ minutes for each group ___ minutes for whole class	**AFTER**

Sample Center Activity Card

Center _____ | Center _____

Date _____ | Date _____

CENTER CARD

Name _____

Center _____ | Center _____

Date _____ | Date _____

Readers' Theater

1. Leader reads the story aloud.

2. Everyone reads the story together.

3. Partners read the story together.

4. Everyone is assigned a part.

5. Students practice their parts on their own.

6. Students practice their parts together.

7. Everyone gets ready to share the story with the class.

Making Words Record Sheet

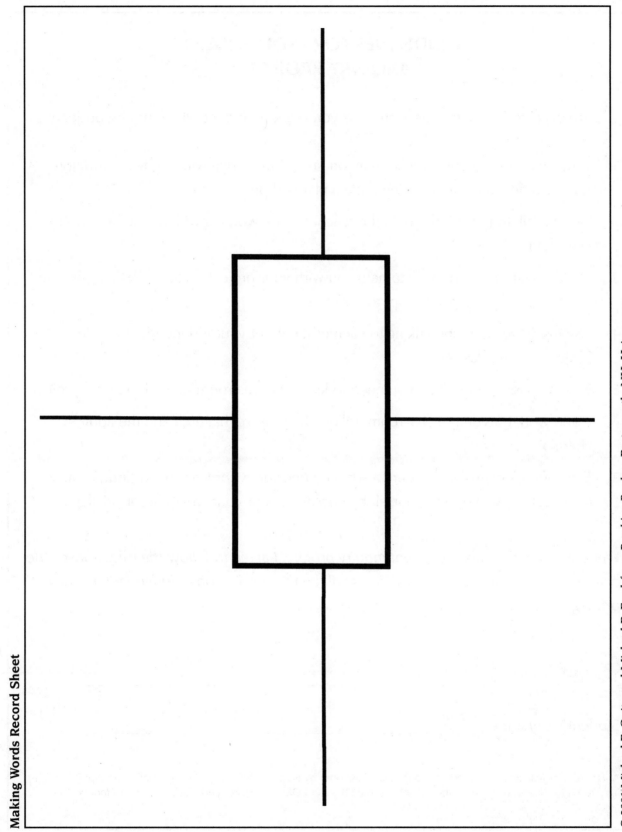

GUIDELINES FOR INDEPENDENT INQUIRY PROJECTS

You are expected to follow these rules as you work on independent inquiry projects:

1. When working on your project, stay on task. Conference with the teacher before starting a new project or setting aside a planned project.

2. Wait to talk to the teacher until the teacher is not working with a group or another classmate.

3. Consult with other students to help you with your project if you are waiting for the teacher, but try not to interrupt their work.

4. Use inside voices when talking to each other about your independent inquiry projects during class time.

5. Use the pass system when you need to leave the classroom to work on your projects.

6. If you work outside the classroom, follow the rules of that area and the adult in charge.

7. Since independent projects are a special opportunity for learning for individuals, avoid calling attention to yourself by boasting about your work and/or privileges.

When working on an independent inquiry project, I agree to follow the rules above. The consequence for not following the rules will be the suspension of independent study privileges.

Teacher's signature _____

Student's signature _____

Adapted from *Teaching Gifted Kids in the Regular Classroom* by Susan Winebrenner (Minneapolis: Free Spirit Publishing, 2001) as suggested by use in the Fort Atkinson (WI) School District *Teacher and Student Guide to Independent Study.*

SPECIAL PROJECT PLANNING SHEET
(PRIMARY GRADES K–2)

Student's name: _____

Date: _____

Special topic: _____

What I want to learn: _____

_____

_____

_____

_____

How I will share what I have learned: _____

_____

_____

_____

_____

_____

Deadline: _____

Adapted from *Teaching Gifted Kids in the Regular Classroom* by Susan Winebrenner (Minneapolis: Free Spirit Publishing, 2001) as suggested by use in the Fort Atkinson (WI) School District *Teacher and Student Guide to Independent Study*.

INDEPENDENT INQUIRY PROJECT PLANNING SHEET
(INTERMEDIATE GRADES 3–5)

Student's name: _____ Date: _____

The topic I have decide to learn more about is _____

My reason for learning more about this topic: _____

_____

_____

Material resources I expect to use in my inquiry: _____

_____

_____

Human resources I expect to use in my inquiry: _____

_____

_____

What I expect to learn from my inquiry: _____

_____

_____

How I expect to share what I have learned: _____

_____

_____

Deadline: _____

Adapted from *Teaching Gifted Kids in the Regular Classroom* by Susan Winebrenner (Minneapolis: Free Spirit Publishing, 2001) as suggested by use in the Fort Atkinson (WI) School District *Teacher and Student Guide to Independent Study.*

Project Format

THIS IS INTERESTING TO ME!

I would like to know about . . .

_____

_____

To learn about this I will . . .

_____

_____

Here's how I will let you know I have learned something . . .

_____

_____

My plan of action is . . .

_____

_____

I will be ready to present it to the class by _____

_____

_____

Student _____

Teacher _____

Adapted from Brenda Wallace, Ashwaubenon, WI.

Student Poem Recordkeeping Grid

Title of Poem:	Title of Poem:	Title of Poem:	Title of Poem:
Read with fluency	Read with fluency	Read with fluency	Read with fluency
Word cards	Word cards	Word cards	Word cards
Word list	Word list	Word list	Word list
Project	Project	Project	Project

Sample Student Punch Card

● ●	● ●	● ●	● ●	● ●
Art Project	Character Cut Out	Read Another Book	Write a letter to the teacher or a friend	Practice for a book talk

● Read with a friend _____'s
●   BOOK RESPONSE CARD   "Showtime" — Group play — Puppets ●
                                                                                                   ●

Poster	Re-make a favorite story	Pop-up	Read into a tape recorder	Book Journal
● ●	● ●	● ●	● ●	● ●

Adapted from *Wisconsin State Reading Association.*

Sample Student Punch Card

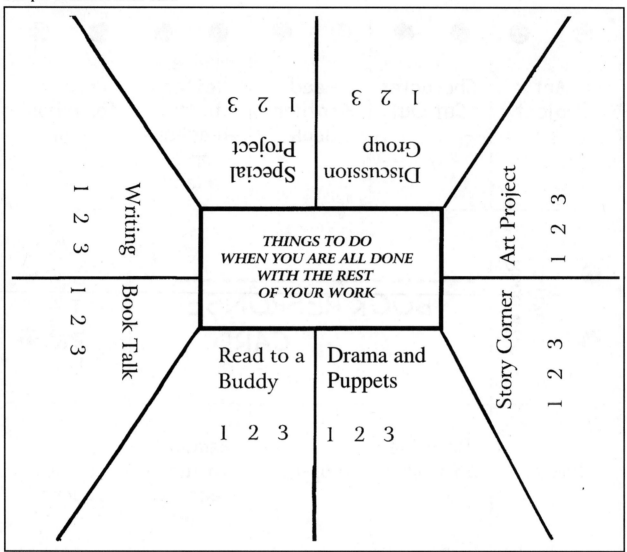

© 2001 Michael F. Opitz and Michael P. Ford from *Reaching Readers*. Portsmouth, NH: Heinemann.

APPENDIX D

Annotated Bibliography of Professional Books

Featured here are some additional references to extend the ideas presented in this book. Other titles can be found throughout this text. Keep in mind that this list is a sampling of the many excellent professional titles currently available.

Chapter 1: Roles and Goals

Books on How Guided Reading Fits into an Overall Reading Program

Booth, D. 1998. *Guiding the Reading Process;* 1996. *Literacy Techniques for Building Successful Readers and Writers.* York, ME: Stenhouse/Pembroke.

> In these two volumes, Canadian educator Booth compiles more than one hundred brief explanations and illustrations of contemporary reading practices, programs, and ideas. A variety of ideas related to guided reading are addressed. Booth also discusses issues and ideas for literature circles and other practices that can help frame and support guided reading instruction.

Calkins, L. 2001. *The Art of Teaching Reading.* New York: Addison Wesley Longman.

> Calkins presents a comprehensive volume focused on reading instruction and includes her perspectives on guided reading practices as one part of the description of ongoing structures in the reading curriculum. Teachers will also find many other sections of Calkins' text useful as they look for insights and ideas to support guided reading instruction.

Cunningham, P., and R. Allington. 1999. *Classrooms That Work: They Can All Read and Write,* 2d ed. New York: Longman.

> The authors take a look at successful classroom reading and writing programs. They look specifically at guided reading as one aspect of programs that work. The authors also describe other aspects of successful reading and writing programs used to support guided reading practices.

*Cunningham, R., D. Hall, and J. Cunningham. 2000. *Guided Reading the Four Blocks Way*. Greensboro, NC: Carson Dellosa.

> After providing an overview of guided reading, the authors provide several classroom vignettes that show how different teachers use guided reading to best meet the needs of their students. Several comprehension strategies are listed and described.

Fountas, I., and G. Pinnell. 1996. *Guided Reading: Good First Teaching for All Children*. Portsmouth, NH: Heinemann.

> Grounded in their work with Reading Recovery, Irene Fountas and Gay Su Pinnell propose guided reading as a way of ensuring good first teaching for all students. Not only does the book provide a research base and a practical framework for guided reading, but it also contains a number of helpful appendices. Teachers will find the extensive list of leveled books an especially helpful starting point. Reproducible forms to support center-based instruction and assessment are also included.

Fountas, I., and G. Pinnell. 2001. *Guiding Readers and Writers Grades 3–6: Teaching Comprehension, Genre, and Content Literacy*. Portsmouth NH: Heinemann.

> Looking at independent reading, literature study, comprehension, word analysis, and the reading–writing connection, in addition to guided reading, Fountas and Pinnell suggest a more comprehensive language and literacy framework for older readers. This resource also includes an extensive list of leveled books for older readers (Levels J–Z). The appendices contain many reproducible forms for instruction and assessments as well as helpful lists (author websites, sources for writer talks, selected fiction, nonfiction, and poetry titles).

Mooney, M. 1990. *Reading To, With, and By Children*. New York: R. C. Owens.

> While this classic volume brought guided reading to our attention, Mooney reminds all teachers of the importance of balance in reading programs—the need to balance guided reading experiences with reading aloud experiences and independent reading opportunities. She offers a brief explanation of these components.

*Routman, R. 2000. *Conversations: Strategies for Teaching, Learning, and Evaluating*. Portsmouth, NH: Heinemann.

> Routman shares her insights and ideas about implementing guided reading as a part of a total reading program. She offers comments encouraging teachers to look at current guided reading instruction critically as they try to improve their practices.

---

*Cited in text.

Chapter 2: Assessment and Grouping

Books on Assessment

Bridges, L. 1996. *Assessment: Continuous Learning*. York, ME: Stenhouse.

> This practical resource offers several teacher-developed ideas that can be used as teachers observe and assess children. The author provides checklists; interview suggestions; and ways to use portfolios, rubrics, and self-evaluation profiles.

*Goodman, Y., and A. Marek. 1996. *Retrospective Miscue Analysis: Revaluing Readers and Reading*. New York: R. C. Owens.

> Designed primarily to assist older struggling readers, Goodman and Marek describe the of Retrospective Miscue Analysis process, which involves readers in identifying, analyzing, and learning from their reading miscues. RMA provides an alternative way to structure guided reading interventions that are more appropriate for older readers.

Johns, J., S. Lenski, and L. Elish-Piper. 1999. *Early Literacy Assessments and Strategies*. Dubuque, IA: Kendall/Hunt.

> This book offers numerous assessment techniques, including directions for adminstrating and scoring each. Accompanying forms can be copied for classroom use. Several specific strategies are also offered.

*Leslie, L., and M. Jett-Simpson. 1997. *Authentic Literacy Assessment: An Ecological Approach*. New York: Longman.

> Using a number of classroom-based examples and teacher voices, Leslie and Jett-Simpson offer a comprehensive description of reading and writing assessment techniques that can be used to gain and document valuable information about students during guided reading experiences.

Books on Grouping

*Caldwell, J., and M. Ford, eds. 1996. *Where Have All the Bluebirds Gone: Transforming Ability-Based Reading Classrooms*. Schofield, WI: Wisconsin State Reading Association.

> In support of the Wisconsin State Reading Association's position statement addressing concerns about grouping practices and the use of ability grouping, this monograph details the research base and rationale for changes in grouping practices. It also provides classroom-based examples of how traditional ability-based reading classrooms were transformed.

*Nagel, G. 2001. *Effective Grouping for Literacy Instruction*. Boston: Allyn and Bacon.

> In this volume, Nagel uses the themes of knowledge, power, and affection in discussing effective grouping practices. She describes circumstances that promote knowledge, power, and affection in

classrooms and practical ideas for how to build each of these with the use of flexible grouping.

*Opitz, M. 1998. *Flexible Grouping in Reading: Practical Ways to Help All Students Become Better Readers*. New York: Scholastic.

> This practical guide addresses understanding flexible grouping basics, selecting texts for flexible groups, planning for successful reading experiences in flexible groups, and assessment progress in flexible grouping. It also offers several forms and formats for teachers to adopt and adapt in their efforts to move forward with flexible grouping.

Chapter 3: Texts

Books

Readance, J., D. Moore, and R. Rickleman eds. 2000. *Prereading Activities for Content Area Reading and Learning,* 3d ed. Newark, DE: International Reading Association.

> This classic volume has been updated and contains ideas for preparing students to read texts, especially in content areas. The authors look at asking and answering questions before reading, forecasting passages, understanding vocabulary, graphically representing information, and writing before reading. Many of these ideas can be adapted by teachers for guided reading experiences.

Szymusiak, K., and F. Sibberson. 2001. *Beyond Leveled Books: Supporting Transitional Readers in Grades 2–5*. Portland, ME: Stenhouse.

> The title captures the essence of this book. The authors provide several titles that can be used to support readers via the way the text is actually written. The book also provides specific examples, minilessons, and bibliographies.

Articles

*Brown, K. 1999/2000. "What Kind of Text—For Whom and When? Textual Scaffolding for Beginning Readers." *The Reading Teacher* 53: 292–307.

> Brown raises an interesting concern about simplistic views of matching readers and texts. She argues for a more complex approach and describes helpful frameworks teachers can use in making decisions about using texts with beginning readers.

Fawson, P., and R. Reutzel. 2000. "But I Only Have a Basal Implementing Guided Reading in the Early Grades." *The Reading Teacher* (September): 84–97.

> Fawson and Reutzel's article provides classroom-based vignettes to demonstrate how commercial basal anthologies can be used in guided reading programs. The article provides an extensive list that

identifies basal selections from some common series books by guided reading levels.

Chapter 4: Instruction

Books on Comprehension Strategies

Blachowicz, C., and D. Ogle. 2001. *Reading Comprehension: Strategies for Independent Learners.* New York: Guilford.

> The book offers a wealth of ideas for fostering comprehension, most of which can be used during guided reading lessons. Ideas are provided for all three phases of guided reading lessons: before, during, and after. The first two chapters explain that all ideas are grounded in research.

Goodman, Y., D. Watson, and C. Burke. 1996. *Reading Strategies: Focus on Comprehension,* 2d ed. New York: R. C. Owens.

> Rooted in the authors' work in miscue analysis, the book presents their view of the reading process and how to make a meaning-focused reading curriculum. They discuss strategies for instruction and evaluation and then present a series of strategy lessons linked to cueing systems.

Harvey. S., and A. Goudvis. 2000. *Strategies That Work: Teaching Comprehension to Enhance Understanding.* Portland: ME: Stenhouse.

> Harvey and Goudvis first discuss how to build a foundation for meaning through strategic thinking, reading, and instruction. Then the authors present a series of comprehension strategies in five key areas: making connections, questioning, visualizing, determining importance, and synthesizing. Three classroom portraits are used to illustrate strategy instruction in context. Teachers may find the appendices describing suggested texts to use in strategy instruction very helpful, as well as the inclusion of a large number of adaptable response formats.

Hoyt, L. 1998. *Revisit, Reflect, Retell: Strategies for Improving Reading Comprehension.* Portsmouth, NH: Heinemann.

> Here is a collection of more than 130 strategies that can be used to help children respond to literature in meaningful ways. The author provides a brief explanation and suggestions for use for each activity and also offers a suggested reproducible when appropriate.

Keene. E. O., and S. Zimmermann. 1997. *Mosaic of Thought: Teaching Comprehension in a Reader's Workshop.* Portsmouth, NH: Heinemann.

> Using a more narrative style, Keene and Zimmermann detail how teachers and students interact to develop more sophisticated understandings of texts. While discussed within the context of reader's

workshop, teachers can gain insights into how to interact with students during shared response guided reading experiences to promote greater understanding of text. Keene and Zimmermann focus on key comprehension strategies: connecting the known to new, determining importance, questioning, sensory imaging, inferring, synthesizing, and independent problem solving.

Books That Focus on Responding to Literature

*Buehl, D. 2001. *Classroom Strategies for Interactive Learning*, 2d ed. Newark, DE: International Reading Association.

> Reading specialist Buehl has compiled more than thirty popular comprehension strategies to use before, during, and after the reading of texts. The use of each strategy is illustrated with a classroom-based example.

Daniels, H. 1994. *Literature Circles: Voice and Choice in the Student-Centered Classroom.* York, ME: Stenhouse.

> Daniels' resource has gained much of its popularity for its definition of roles students can be assigned or assume to help structure discussions in small groups. Daniels even includes role sheets in both English and Spanish, which can be easily reproduced or modified for classroom use with younger and older readers.

*Donoghue, M. 2001. *Using Literature Activities to Teach Content Areas to Emergent Readers.* Boston: Allyn and Bacon.

> Donoghue looks at content standards in science, social studies and mathematics as defined by related national organizations. Then she identifies a number of links with literature (content standard, book, and activity) that can be used to promote content area understandings with young children. This resource might be most helpful for teachers working to bridge connections between content areas and guided reading.

*Gambrell, L., and J. Almasi, eds. 1996. *Lively Discussions! Fostering Engaged Reading.* Newark, DE: International Reading Association.

> Another edited volume representing a number of voices on the importance of discussion in reading programs. Grounded in the work of the National Reading Research Center, teachers will add to their techniques and strategies for effectively using discussion as a tool for learning in guided reading experiences.

McMahon, S., and T. Raphael, eds. (with L. Goatley and L. Pardo). 1997. *The Book Club Connection.* Newark, DE: International Reading Association.

> McMahon and Raphael use teacher voices to show how their Book Club program can be implemented in classrooms. Book Club provides a framework that can inform teachers' thinking as they plan for shared response guided reading experiences.

Paratore, J., and R. McCormack, eds. 1997. *Peer Talk in the Classroom: Learning from Research.* Newark, DE: International Reading Association.

This edited volume focuses primarily on peer-led book discussions. Using the voices of a number of university- and classroom-based researchers, this resource looks at how teachers can turn control for book discussions over to students, what happens when students take control of book discussions, and how teachers can work behind the scenes to enhance the quality of student interactions about books.

Parks, S., and H. Black. 1990/1992. *Organizing Thinking, Book I and Book II.* Pacific Grove, CA: Critical Thinking Press.

Designed for critical thinking work with gifted students, these resources contain an extensive number of reproducible graphic organizers to use for increasingly sophisticated processing of texts and reflection on texts. Some are specifically designed for language arts lessons, but others are linked to content area instruction in social studies, mathematics, science, and fine arts. One section of each resource even introduces students to organizers to help with personal problem solving.

Peterson, R., and M. Eeds. 1990. *Grand Conversations: Literature Groups in Action.* New York: Scholastic.

This small volume was one of the first to capture the importance of literature-based programs as a vehicle for children to read and respond to books through dialogue and discussion. Peterson and Eeds have identified a list of key literary elements that can form the heart of guided reading demonstrations and interventions.

Roser, N., and M. Martinez, eds. 1995. *Book Talk and Beyond: Children and Teachers Respond to Literature.* Newark, DE: International Reading Association.

Roser and Martinez have also assembled a collection of voices to discuss the role of talk in classroom reading programs. Divided into four sections—getting ready for story talk, the tools of story talk, guiding book talks, and other responses to literature—the authors use a number of classroom-based examples to illustrate ideas that teachers can consider in planning activities for and around guided reading.

Short, K. G., and K. M. Pierce, eds. 1990. *Talking About Books: Creating Literate Communities.* Portsmouth, NH: Heinemann.

This edited volume contains a number of perspectives on establishing literature-based reading programs. While it predates the popularity of guided reading, teachers may want to revisit this resource to gain insights and ideas for shared response guided reading groups, especially as readers grow in competency and sophistication.

Wisconsin Department of Public Instruction. 1989. *Strategic Learning in the Content Areas.* Madison, WI: Author.

> The Wisconsin Department of Public Instruction publishes this popular guide for how effective strategy instruction should transcend reading programs and impact teaching and learning in the content areas. Most helpful to content teachers is the inclusion of two dozen strategies that can be easily modified for content lesson instruction.

Wood, K. 2001. *Literacy Strategies Across the Subject Area: Process-Oriented Blackline Masters for the K–12 Classroom.* Boston: Allyn and Bacon.

> Wood has compiled two dozen strategy and response activities that can be used by teachers to support guided reading instruction and/ or to frame independent activity for students away from the teacher.

Books That Focus on Word Identification Strategies

Cunningham, P. 2000. *Phonics They Use: Words for Reading and Writing,* 3d ed. New York: Longman.

> This practical guide provides an endless supply of classroom ideas for integration into guided reading demonstrations and interventions. Patricia Cunningham devotes the final quarter of her resource to identifying ideas for working with big words—multisyllabic words—which might be most useful for teachers of more sophisticated and competent readers.

Ganske, K. 2000. *Word Journeys: Assessment-Guided Phonics, Spelling, and Vocabulary Instruction.* New York: Guilford.

> Ganske's resource is another thorough look at word identification instruction. She devotes a significant section of this resource to helping teachers assess students' needs. Teachers will find many ideas for planning assessment-based instruction for early skills, such as letter names and within word patterns, as well as more sophisticated skills related to syllable junctures and derivational constancy. Ganske includes an extensive collection of supplemental word lists that teachers may find useful in planning word identification lessons. She also includes a number of reproducible forms that can be used to support word identification activities.

Gunning, T. 2000. *Building Words: A Resource Manual for Teaching Word Analysis and Spelling Strategies.* Boston: Allyn and Bacon.

> Gunning provides a comprehensive, practical look at word identification instruction, which can be used to support guided reading instruction with and away from the teacher. Gunning discusses how teachers can assess students' literacy development. He provides specific instructional ideas for teaching phonics, vowel patterns, sight words, syllabic analysis, using context, and spelling. Then, he describes an overall plan for bringing the elements together, including

an assessment tool based on benchmark passages and a number of reproducible fold-and-read books in his appendices.

Pinnell, G., and I. Fountas. 1998. *Word Matters: Teaching Phonics and Spelling in the Reading/Writing Classroom.* Portsmouth, NH: Heinemann.
> Described as a companion volume to *Guided Reading*, Pinnell and Fountas outline a word study program to integrate into a balanced reading program. Teachers may find the large number of resource lists, reproducible forms, and other appendices most helpful in adapting ideas for their program.

Wagstaff, J. 1999. *Teaching Reading and Writing with Word Walls.* New York: Scholastic.
> With the increasing presence of word walls in classrooms, it seems natural to use them as a center for independent activity during guided reading instruction. This practical guide provides a number of activities that can be used in turning the word wall into an independent instructional center.

Books on Related Classroom Practices

McCarrier, A., G. Pinnell, and I. Fountas. 2000. *Interactive Writing: How Language and Literacy Come Together, K–2.* Portsmouth, NH: Heinemann.
> Also identified as a companion to *Guided Reading*, this resource presents a comprehensive program for integrating interactive writing into a balanced reading program. Interactive writing provides a practical framework to support guided reading and instructional experiences away from the teacher.

Opitz, M., and T. Rasinski. 1998. *Good-Bye Round Robin: 25 Effective Oral Reading Strategies.* Portsmouth, NH: Heinimann.
> Oral reading still plays a critical role in guided reading experiences. Within classroom-based lessons, Opitz and Rasinski provide teachers with many ways to incorporate oral reading without relying on round-robin reading.

Chapter 5: Organization and Management

Books That Focus on Learner Centers and Independent Literacy Activities

Allen, I., and S. Peery. 2000. *Literacy Centers, Grades 3–5.* Huntington Beach, CA: Creative Teaching Press.
> The majority of this book describes specific learning centers along with reproducibles that can be used in them. The authors provide primary objectives, suggestions for setup and management, and additional tips for each center. Activities are organized around multiple intelligences. Management, assessment, and accountability are also briefly addressed.

Finney, S. 2000. *Keep the Rest of the Class Reading and Writing . . . While You Teach Small Groups.* New York: Scholastic.

> Finney takes on the most frequent question teachers ask, "What do I do with the rest of the class?" This very practical guide presents sixty ideas and reproducible formats teachers can consider in designing independent work to engage students while away from the teacher.

*Harvey, S. 1998. *Nonfiction Matters: Reading, Writing, and Research in Grades 3–8.* York: ME: Stenhouse.

> Harvey presents classroom-based examples of how independent individual inquiry projects can be used with older students to guide their learning away from the teacher.

Helm, J. H., and L. Katz. 2001. *Young Investigators: The Project Approach in the Early Years.* New York: Teachers' College Press.

> Although designed for and popular with early childhood programs, the Project Approach provides a framework for designing independent learning activities for younger students. Helm and Katz include useful reproducible forms and formats to walk teachers (and their students) through each step of the process.

Opitz, M. 1994. *Learning Centers: Getting Them Started, Keeping Them Going.* New York: Scholastic.

> Opitz has put together a very practical guide to help teachers think through learning centers, including how to set them up, build in accountability, and organize them in a classroom schedule. He includes many useful forms and formats to assist teachers in designing centers to support instruction away from the teacher during guided reading time.

Books That Focus on Classroom Organization

Bridges, L. 1996. *Creating Your Classroom Community.* York, ME: Stenhouse.

> This book offers specific suggestions for how to create classrooms that support children as learners and as members of the larger community. It also provides ideas for helping children become responsible learners.

Dorn, L., C. French, and T. Jones. 1998. *Apprenticeship in Literacy: Transitions Across Reading and Writing.* York, ME: Stenhouse.

> Using their background as Reading Recovery teachers and trainers, the authors describe a balanced reading program for primary classrooms. One chapter focuses on the role of guided reading, whereas other chapters describe practices that can be used to support guided reading. Teachers will find the chapter on establishing routines and organizing the classroom very helpful.

Feldman, J. 1997. *Wonderful Rooms Where Children Can Bloom!* (K–2). Peterborough, NH: Crystal Springs.

> Here's a book that offers a wealth of ideas for engaging children with meaningful, independent activities. Suggestions for using every conceivable surface in the classroom to display activities are provided. Suggested matierals, directions, and variations are described for each activity.

Soderman, A., K. Gregory, and L. O'Neill. 1999. *Scaffolding Emergent Literacy: A Child-Centered Approach for Preschool Through Grade 5*. New York: Allyn and Bacon.

> This resource offers a comprehensive look at early literacy programs. After discussing child development and literacy, the authors describe how to create a supportive, nurturing environment.

Taberski, S. 2000. *On Solid Ground: Strategies for Teaching K–3*. Portsmouth, NH: Heinemann.

> Using her classroom experiences, the author describes her goals, classroom envrionment, daily schedule, assessment techniques, instructional strategies, and classroom routines as a way of providing insights and ideas for others.

Index

guided reading in reading program, 3
learning centers (*see* Learning
    centers)
learning to read by reading, 3
Reading and Writing Literacy Genres, 42
Reading and Writing the Room
    learning center, 89–90
Reading attitude survey for grades 3-6,
    120–21, 129
Reading Teacher, The, 33, 39
Reading To, With, and By Students, 1
Recent Newbery award and honor books, 41
Recorded readings, 101
Recordkeeping, independent study
    and, 99–102, 154
Red Leaf, Yellow Leaf, 29
Reilly-Giff, Patricia, 39, 42
Rereading text, 4
Research proposal, 97
Resources, considering, 48
Responding through art learning
    centers, 93
Response journals, 101
Retelling, 4, 120, 127
Revising guided reading, 6–9
Role playing, 85
Roles, bibliography for, 157–58
Rotation schedule for learning centers,
    105–07
Routines, learning centers and class,
    86–87, 147
Rowling, J. K., 39
Ruby Bridges, 43
Running record, 118–19, 123–24
Rylant, Cynthia, 41, 42

S
Scaffolding
    expanding literacy growth using,
        12–13
    as reason for using variety of texts,
        29
Scavenger hunts, 90
Scholastic News, 44
Sees Behind Trees, 42
Self-extending systems
    developing, 4
    expanding ability to develop, 10
Series books, 38–40
*Serpent's Tongue, The: Prose, Poetry, and
    Art of the New Mexico Pueblos*, 42
Sesame Street Magazine, 43
Shared response, 50
    first grade scenario involving, 50–52
    second grade scenario involving,
        57–59, 141–42

fourth grade scenario involving,
    61–63
fifth grade combination scenarios
    involving, 64, 67–72, 143
sixth grade scenario involving, 75–80,
    144–45
sixth grade combination scenario
    involving, 73–75
grouping for, 19, 20, 21
Sharing, of management and account-
    ability tasks, 102
Shiloh, 41, 69–72
Silverstein, Shel, 93
Similar achievement, 22
Skill grouping, 23
Small group instruction, 6, 24, 26, 27
    acceptable texts used for, 12
    moving from large to small groups,
        50–52
    organization and management for
        (*see* Learning centers; Organization
        and management)
    value of, 82
Space concerns, learning centers and,
    104–05
Spaghetti, 93
Special needs students, learning centers
    and, 107–09
Special projects planning sheet (grades
    K-2), 94–95, 151
Steig, William, 42
Story maps, 57, 58, 141–42
Story packs learning centers, 91
Strategies
    determing the purpose for guided
        reading experience, 46, 47
    modeling reading, 4, 64, 65
    modeling strategies good readers
        use, 64, 65
Structured focus workshops, 75
Student interview, 121, 130
Sunshine Series, The, 30

T
Taylor, Mildred, 43
*Teach a Child to Read with Children's
    Books*, 35
Teacher preparation, learning centers
    and, 86
Teachers
    effective practices, enabling teachers
        to expand use of, 11
    role of, as guided reading perspec-
        tive, 6
Teacher-student interaction, 101–02
Teaching Poetry: Yes, You Can!, 40